A Bunch of Everlasting; or, Texts that Made History

F. W. Boreham

BIBLIOLIFE

A BUNCH
OF EVERLASTINGS

OR

TEXTS THAT MADE HISTORY

A VOLUME OF SERMONS

BY

F. W. BOREHAM

AUTHOR OF

"A REEL OF RAINBOW"; "THE UTTERMOST STAR"; "THE SILVER SHADOW",
"THE OTHER SIDE OF THE HILL"; "FACES IN THE FIRE"; "MUSHROOMS
ON THE MOOR", "THE GOLDEN MILESTONE"; "MOUNTAINS
IN THE MIST"; "THE LUGGAGE OF LIFE," ETC.

"There still is need for martyrs and apostles,
There still are texts for never-dying song."
—*Lowell.*

THE ABINGDON PRESS

NEW YORK   CINCINNATI

CONTENTS

PAGE

By Way of Introduction.................. 5

I. Thomas Chalmers' Text.................. 7

II. Martin Luther's Text.... 18

III. Sir John Franklin's Text................. 28

IV. Thomas Boston's Text..................... 39

V. Hugh Latimer's Text...................... 51

VI. John Bunyan's Text....................... 62

VII. Sir Walter Scott's Text 73

VIII. Oliver Cromwell's Text.................. 83

IX. Francis Xavier's Text.................... 92

X. J. B. Gough's Text...................... 99

XI. John Knox's Text..... 110

XII. William Cowper's Text.................. 120

XIII. David Livingstone's Text................. 129

XIV. C. H. Spurgeon's Text.................. 141

XV. Dean Stanley's Text...................... 150

Contents

		PAGE
XVI.	WILLIAM CAREY'S TEXT	161
XVII.	JAMES HANNINGTON'S TEXT	173
XVIII.	WILLIAM WILBERFORCE'S TEXT	185
XIX.	JOHN WESLEY'S TEXT	198
XX.	WILLIAM KNIBB'S TEXT	210
XXI.	JOHN NEWTON'S TEXT	222
XXII.	ANDREW FULLER'S TEXT	235
XXIII.	STEPHEN GRELLET'S TEXT	247

BY WAY OF INTRODUCTION

FIVE AND TWENTY years ago to-night I was solemnly ordained a minister of the everlasting gospel. A medley of most romantic circumstances conspired to fix indelibly upon my mind the profound impressions then created. I was a total stranger on this side of the planet: I had only landed in New Zealand a few hours before. Yet here I was among a people who were pleased to recognise in me their first minister! Trembling under the consciousness of my boyish inexperience, and shuddering under the awful burden imposed upon me by the Ordination Charge, I felt that life had suddenly become tremendous. I was doing business in deep waters! As a recognition of the goodness and mercy that have followed me all the days of my ministerial life, I desire, with inexpressible thankfulness, to send forth this Bunch of Everlastings.

FRANK W. BOREHAM.

ARMADALE, MELBOURNE, AUSTRALIA.
March 15th, 1920.

I

THOMAS CHALMERS' TEXT

I

IT was a mystery. Nobody in Kilmany could understand it. They were people of the flock and the field, men of the plough and the pasture. There were only about one hundred and fifty families scattered across the parish, and such social life as they enjoyed all circled round the kirk. They were all very fond of their young minister, and very proud of his distinguished academic attainments. Already, in his preaching, there were hints of that 'sublime thunder' that afterwards rolled through the world. In his later years it was said of him that Scotland shuddered beneath his billowy eloquence as a cathedral vibrates to the deep notes of the organ. He became, as Lord Rosebery has testified, the most illustrious Scotsman since John Knox. But his farmer-folk at Kilmany could not be expected to foresee all this. They felt that their minister was no ordinary man; yet there was one thing about him that puzzled every member of the congregation. The drovers talked of it as they met each other on the long and lonely roads; the women discussed it as they waited outside the kirk whilst

7

their husbands harnessed up the horses; the
farmers themselves referred to it wonderingly
when they talked things over in the stockyards and
the market-place. Mr. Chalmers was only twenty-
three. He had matriculated at twelve; had become
a divinity student at fifteen; and at nineteen had
been licensed to preach. Now that, with much
fear and trembling, he had settled at Kilmany, he
made a really excellent minister. He has himself
told us that, as he rode about his parish, his affections flew before him. He loved to get to the
firesides of the people, and he won from old and
young their unstinted admiration, their confidence
and their love. But for all that, the mystery
remained. Briefly stated, it was this: Why did
he persist in preaching to these decent, well-
meaning and law-abiding Scottish farmers in a
strain that implied that they ought all to be in
gaol? Why, Sabbath after Sabbath, did he thunder at them concerning the heinous wickedness
of theft, of murder, and of adultery? After a hard
week's work in field and stable, byre and dairy,
these sturdy Scotsmen drove to the kirk at the
sound of the Sabbath bell, only to find themselves
rated by the minister as though they had spent
the week in open shame! They filed into their
family pews with their wives and their sons and
their daughters, and were straightway charged
with all the crimes in the calendar! Later on, the
minister himself saw both the absurdity and the

pity of it. It was, as he told the good people of Kilmany, part of his bitter self-reproach that, for the greater part of the time he spent among them, 'I could expatiate only on the meanness of dishonesty, on the villany of falsehood, on the despicable arts of calumny, in a word, upon all those deformities of character which awaken the natural indignation of the human heart against the pests and disturbers of human society.' Now and again, the brilliant and eloquent young preacher turned aside from this line of things in order to denounce the designs of Napoleon. But as the Fifeshire farmers saw no way in which the arguments of their minister were likely to come under the notice of the tyrant and turn him from his fell purpose of invading Britain, they were as much perplexed by these sermons as by the others. This kind of thing continued without a break from 1803 until 1811 ; and the parish stood bewildered.

II

From 1803 until 1811! But what of the four years that followed? For he remained at Kilmany until 1815—the year of Waterloo! Let me set a second picture beside the one I have already painted! Could any contrast be greater? The people were bewildered before: they were even more bewildered now! The minister was another man: the kirk was another place! During those closing years at Kilmany, Mr. Chalmers thundered

against the grosser crimes no more. He never
again held forth from his pulpit against the in-
iquities of the Napoleonic programme. But every
Sunday he had something fresh to say about the
love of God, about the Cross of Christ, and about
the way of salvation. Every Sunday he urged his
people with tears to repent, to believe, and to
enter into life everlasting. Every Sunday he set
before them the beauty of the Christian life, and,
by all the arts of eloquent persuasion, endeavoured
to lead his people into it. 'He would bend over
the pulpit,' writes one who heard him both before
and after the change, 'he would bend over the
pulpit and press us to take the gift, as if he held
it that moment in his hand and would not be satisfied till every one of us had got possession of
it. And often, when the sermon was over, and
the psalm was sung, and he rose to pronounce the
blessing, he would break out afresh with some new
entreaty, unwilling to let us go until he had made
one more effort to persuade us to accept it.' Now
here are the two pictures side by side—the picture
of Chalmers during his first eight years at Kilmany,
and the picture of Chalmers during his last four
years there! The question is: What happened in
1811 to bring about the change?

III

That is the question; and the answer, bluntly
stated, is that, in 1811, Chalmers was converted!

He made a startling discovery—the most sensational discovery that any man ever made. He had occupied all the years of his ministry on the Ten Commandments; he now discovered, not only that there are more commandments than ten, but that the greatest commandments of all are not to be found among the ten! The experience of Chalmers resembles in many respects the experience of the Marquis of Lossie. Readers of George Macdonald's *Malcolm* will never forget the chapter on 'The Marquis and the Schoolmaster.' The dying marquis sends for the devout schoolmaster, Mr. Graham. The schoolmaster knows his man, and goes cautiously to work.

'Are you satisfied with yourself, my lord?'

'No, by God!'

'You would like to be better?'

'Yes; but how is a poor devil to get out of this infernal scrape?'

'Keep the commandments!'

'That's it, of course; but there's no time!'

'If there were but time to draw another breath, there would be time to begin!'

'How am I to begin? Which am I to begin with?'

'There is one commandment which includes all the rest!'

'Which is that?'

'*Believe on the Lord Jesus Christ and thou shalt be saved!*'

When the Marquis of Lossie passed from the ten commandments to the commandment that includes all the ten, he found the peace for which he hungered, and, strangely enough, Chalmers entered into life in a precisely similar way.

IV

'I am much taken,' he says in his journal, in May, 1811, 'I am much taken with Walker's observation that we are *commanded* to believe on the Son of God!'

Commanded!

The Ten Commandments!

The Commandment that includes all the Commandments!

'*Believe on the Lord Jesus Christ and thou shalt be saved!*'

That was the Marquis of Lossie's text, and it was Chalmers'.

At about this time, he was overtaken by a serious illness. He always regarded those days of feebleness and confinement as the critical days in his spiritual history. Long afterwards, when the experience of the years had shown that the impressions then made were not transitory, he wrote to his brother giving him an account of the change that then overtook him. He describes it as a great revolution in all his methods of thought. 'I am now most thoroughly of opinion,' he goes on, 'that on the system of "Do this and live!" no peace can ever be attained. It is *"Believe on the Lord Jesus Christ and thou shalt be saved!"* When this belief enters the heart, joy and confidence enter along with it!'

'Thus,' says Dr. Hanna in his great biography of Chalmers, 'thus we see him stepping from the treacherous ground of "Do and live!" to place his feet upon the firm foundation of *"Believe on the Lord Jesus Christ and thou shalt be saved!"* '

Do!—The Ten Commandments—that was his theme at Kilmany for eight long years!

Believe!—The Commandment that includes all the Commandments—that was the word that transformed his life and transfigured his ministry!

'Believe on the Lord Jesus Christ and thou shalt be saved!'

V

The result of that change we have partly seen. But only partly. We have seen it from the point of view of *the pew*. We have seen the farmer-folk of Kilmany astonished as they caught a new note in the minister's preaching, a new accent in the minister's voice. But we must see the change from the point of view of *the pulpit*. And, as seen from the pulpit, the result of the transformation was even more surprising and sensational. Chalmers alone can tell that story, and we must let him tell it in his own way. The twelve years at Kilmany— the eight *before* the change, and the four *after* it—

have come to an end at last; and, at a special meeting called for the purpose, Mr. Chalmers is taking a sorrowful farewell of his first congregation. The farmers and their wives have driven in from far and near. Their minister has been called to a great city charge; they are proud of it; but they find it hard to give him up. The valedictory speeches have all been made, and now Mr. Chalmers rises to reply. After a feeling acknowledgement of the compliments paid him, he utters one of the most impressive and valuable testimonies to which any minister ever gave expression. 'I cannot but record,' he says, 'the effect of an actual though undesigned experiment which I prosecuted for upwards of twelve years among you. For the first eight years of that time I could expatiate only on the meanness of dishonesty, on the villany of falsehood, on the despicable arts of calumny, in a word, upon all those deformities of character which awaken the natural indignation of the human heart against the pests and disturbers of human society. But the interesting fact is, that, during the whole of that period, I never once heard of any reformation being wrought amongst my people. All the vehemence with which I urged the virtues and the proprieties of social life had not the weight of a feather on the moral habits of my parishioners. It was not until the free offer of forgiveness through the blood of Christ was urged upon the acceptance of my hearers that I ever heard of any of those subordinate reformations which I made the ultimate object of my earlier ministrations.' And he closes that farewell speech with these memorable words: 'You have taught me,' he says, 'that to preach Christ is the only effective way of preaching morality; and out of your humble cottages I have gathered a lesson which, in all its simplicity, I shall carry into a wider theatre.'

Do!—The Ten Commandments—that was his theme at Kilmany for eight long years, and it had not the weight of a feather!

Believe!—The Commandment that includes all the Commandments—that was his theme for the last four years, and he beheld its gracious and renovating effects in every home in the parish!

'Believe on the Lord Jesus Christ and thou shalt be saved!'

With that great witness on his lips, Chalmers lays down his charge at Kilmany, and plunges into a larger sphere to make world-history!

VI

'Believe on the Lord Jesus Christ and thou shalt be saved!' Chalmers greatly believed and was greatly saved. He was saved from all sin and made saintly. 'If ever a halo surrounded a saint,' declares Lord Rosebery, 'it encompassed Chalmers!' He was saved from all littleness and made great. Mr. Gladstone used to say of him that the world can never forget 'his warrior

grandeur, his unbounded philanthropy, his strength
of purpose, his mental integrity, his absorbed and
absorbing earnestness; and, above all, his singular
simplicity; he was one of nature's nobles.' 'A strong
featured man,' said Carlyle, thinking of the massive
form, the leonine head and the commanding countenance of his old friend; 'a strong featured man,
and of very beautiful character.' When I want a
definition of the salvation that comes by faith, I
like to think of Thomas Chalmers.

VII

Yes; he greatly believed and was greatly saved;
he greatly lived and greatly died. It is a Sunday
evening. He—now an old man of sixty-seven—has
remained at home, and has spent a delightful evening with his children and grandchildren. It is one
of the happiest evenings that they have ever spent
together. 'We had family worship this morning,'
the old doctor says to a minister who happens to
be present, 'but you must give us worship again
this evening. I expect to give worship in the
morning!' Immediately after prayers he withdraws,
smiling and waving his hands to them all and
wishing them, 'a general good-night!' They call
him in the morning: but there is no response. *'I
expect to give worship in the morning!'* he had said;
and he has gone to give it! He is sitting up in bed,
half erect, his head reclining gently on the pillow;
the expression of his countenance that of fixed and

majestic repose. His students liked to think that their old master had been translated at the zenith of his powers: he felt no touch of senile decay.

'Believe on the Lord Jesus Christ and thou shalt be saved!' What is it to be saved? I do not know. No man knows. But as I think of the transformation that the text effected in the experience of Chalmers; as I contemplate his valiant and unselfish life; together with his beautiful and glorious death; and as I try to conceive of the felicity into which that Sunday night he entered, I can form an idea.

II

MARTIN LUTHER'S TEXT

I

It goes without saying that the text that made Martin Luther made history with a vengeance. When, through its mystical but mighty ministry, Martin Luther entered into newness of life, the face of the world was changed. It was as though all the windows of Europe had been suddenly thrown open, and the sunshine came streaming in everywhere. The destinies of empires were turned that day into a new channel. Carlyle has a stirring and dramatic chapter in which he shows that every nation under heaven stood or fell according to the attitude that it assumed towards Martin Luther. 'I call this Luther a true Great Man,' he exclaims. 'He is great in intellect, great in courage, great in affection and integrity; one of our most lovable and gracious men. He is great, not as a hewn obelisk is great, but as an Alpine mountain is great; so simple, honest, spontaneous; not setting himself up to be great, but there for quite another purpose than the purpose of being great!' 'A mighty man,' he says again; what were all emperors, popes and potentates in comparison? His light was to flame as a beacon over long centuries and epochs of the world; the whole world and its history was waiting for this man!' And elsewhere he declares that the moment in which Luther defied the wrath of the Diet of Worms was the greatest moment in the modern history of men. Here, then, was *the man;* what was *the text* that made him?

II

Let us visit a couple of very interesting European libraries! And here, in the Convent Library at Erfurt, we are shown an exceedingly famous and beautiful picture. It represents Luther as a young monk of four and twenty, poring in the early morning over a copy of the Scriptures to which a bit of broken chain is hanging. The dawn is stealing through the open lattice, illumining both the open Bible and the eager face of its reader. And on the page that the young monk so intently studies are to be seen the words: '*The just shall live by faith.*'

'*The just shall live by faith!*'

'*The just shall live by faith!*'

These, then, are the words that made the world all over again. And now, leaving the Convent Library at Erfurt, let us visit another library, the Library of Rudolstadt! For here, in a glass case, we shall discover a manuscript that will fascinate us. It is a letter in the handwriting of Dr. Paul Luther, the reformer's youngest son. 'In the year 1544,' we read, 'my late dearest father, in the presence of us all, narrated the whole story of his journey to Rome. He acknowledged with great joy that, in that city, through the Spirit of Jesus Christ, he had come to the knowledge of the truth of the everlasting gospel. It happened in this way. As he repeated his prayers on the Lateran staircase, the words of the Prophet Habakkuk came suddenly to his mind: *"The just shall live by faith."* Thereupon he ceased his prayers, returned to Wittenberg, and took this as the chief foundation of all his doctrine.'

'The just shall live by faith!'
'The just shall live by faith!'

The picture in the one library, and the manuscript in the other, have told us all that we desire to know.

III

'The just shall live by faith!'
'The just shall live by faith!'

The words do not flash or glitter. Like the ocean, they do not give any indication upon the surface of the profundities and mysteries that lie concealed beneath. And yet of what other text can it be said that, occurring in the Old Testament, it is thrice quoted in the New?

'The just shall live by faith!' cries the Prophet.

'The just shall live by faith!' says Paul, when he addresses a letter to the greatest of the European churches.

'The just shall live by faith!' he says again, in his letter to the greatest of the Asiatic churches.

'The just shall live by faith!' says the writer of the Epistle to the Hebrews, addressing himself to Jews.

It is as though it were the sum and substance of everything, to be proclaimed by prophets in the old dispensation, and echoed by apostles in the new; to be translated into all languages and transmitted to every section of the habitable earth. Indeed, Bishop Lightfoot as good as says that the words represent the concentration and epitome of all revealed religion. 'The whole law,' he says, 'was given to Moses in six hundred and thirteen precepts. David, in the fifteenth Psalm, brings them all within the compass of eleven. Isaiah reduces them to six; Micah to three; and Isaiah, in a later passage, to two. But Habakkuk condenses them all into one: *"The just shall live by faith!"* '

And this string of monosyllables that sums up everything and is sent to everybody—the old world's text: the new world's text: the prophet's text: the Jew's text: the European's text: the Asiatic's text: everybody's text—is, in a special and peculiar sense, Martin Luther's text. We made that discovery in the libraries of Erfurt and Rudolstadt; and we shall, as we proceed, find abundant evidence to confirm us in that conclusion.

IV

For, strangely enough, the text that echoed itself three times in the New Testament, echoed itself three times also in the experience of Luther. It met him at Wittenberg, it met him at Bologna, and it finally mastered him at Rome.

It was at Wittenberg that the incident occurred which we have already seen transferred to the painter's canvas. In the retirement of his quiet cell, while the world is still wrapped in slumber, he pores over the epistle to the Romans. Paul's quotation from Habakkuk strangely captivates him.

'The just shall live by faith!'

'The just shall live by faith!'

'This precept,' says the historian, 'fascinates him. "For the just, then," he says to himself, "there is a life different from that of other men; and this life is the gift of faith!" This promise, to which he opens all his heart, as if God had placed it there specially for him, unveils to him the mystery of the Christian life. For years afterwards, in the midst of his numerous occupations, he fancies that he still hears the words repeating themselves to him over and over again.'

'The just shall live by faith!'

'The just shall live by faith!'

Years pass. Luther travels. In the course of his journey, he crosses the Alps, is entertained at a Benedictine Convent at Bologna, and is there overtaken by a serious sickness. His mind relapses into utmost darkness and dejection. To die thus, under a burning sky and in a foreign land! He shudders at the thought. 'The sense of his sinfulness troubles him; the prospect of judgement fills him with dread. But at the very moment at which these terrors reach their highest pitch, the words that had already struck him at Wittenberg recur forcibly to his memory and enlighten his soul like a ray from heaven—

"The just shall live by faith!"
"The just shall live by faith!"

Thus restored and comforted,' the record concludes, 'he soon regains his health and resumes his journey.'

The third of these experiences—the experience narrated in that fireside conversation of which the manuscript at Rudolstadt has told us—befalls him at Rome. 'Wishing to obtain an indulgence promised by the Pope to all who shall ascend Pilate's Staircase on their knees, the good Saxon monk is painfully creeping up those steps which, he is told, were miraculously transported from Jerusalem to Rome. Whilst he is performing this meritorious act, however, he thinks he hears a voice of thunder crying, as at Wittenberg and Bologna—

"The just shall live by faith!"
"The just shall live by faith!"

'These words, that twice before have struck him

like the voice of an angel from heaven, resound unceasingly and powerfully within him. He rises in amazement from the steps up which he is dragging his body: he shudders at himself: he is ashamed at seeing to what a depth superstition plunged him. He flies far from the scene of his folly.'

Thus, thrice in the New Testament and thrice in the life of Luther, the text speaks with singular appropriateness and effect.

V

'This powerful text,' remarks Merle D'Aubigné, 'has a mysterious influence on the life of Luther. It was a *creative sentence,* both for the reformer and for the Reformation. It was in these words that God then said, "Let there be light!" and there was light!'

VI

It was the unveiling of the Face of God! Until this great transforming text flashed its light into the soul of Luther, his thought of God was a pagan thought. And the pagan thought is an unjust thought, an unworthy thought, a cruel thought. Look at this Indian devotee! From head to foot he bears the marks of the torture that he has inflicted upon his body in his frantic efforts to give pleasure to his god. His back is a tangle of scars. The flesh has been lacerated by the pitiless hooks by which he has swung himself on the terrible churuka. Iron spears have been repeatedly run through his tongue. His ears are torn to ribbons. What does it mean? It can only mean that he worships a fiend! His god loves to see him in anguish! His cries of pain are music in the ears of the deity whom he adores! This ceaseless orgy of torture is his futile endeavour to satisfy the idol's lust for blood. Luther made precisely the same mistake. To his sensitive mind, every thought of God was a thing of terror. 'When I was young,' he tells us, 'it happened that at Eisleben, on Corpus Christi day, I was walking with the procession, when, suddenly, the sight of the Holy Sacrament which was carried by Doctor Staupitz, so terrified me that a cold sweat covered my body and I believed myself dying of terror.' All through his convent days he proceeds upon the assumption that God gloats over his misery. His life is a long drawn out agony. He creeps like a shadow along the galleries of the cloister, the walls echoing with his dismal moanings. His body wastes to a skeleton; his strength ebbs away: on more than one occasion his brother monks find him prostrate on the convent floor and pick him up for dead. And all the time he thinks of God as One who can find delight in these continuous torments! The just shall live, he says to himself, by penance and by pain. The just shall live by fasting: the just shall live by fear.

VII

'The just shall live by fear!' Luther mutters to himself every day of his life.

'The just shall live by faith!' says the text that breaks upon him like a light from heaven.

'By fear! By fear!'

'By faith! By faith!'

And what is faith? The theologians may find difficulty in defining it, yet every little child knows what it is. In all the days of my own ministry I have found only one definition that has satisfied me, and whenever I have had occasion to speak of faith, I have recited it. It is Bishop O'Brien's:—

'They who know what is meant by faith in a promise, know what is meant by faith in the Gospel; they who know what is meant by faith in a remedy, know what is meant by faith in the blood of the Redeemer; they who know what is meant by faith in a physician, faith in an advocate, faith in a friend, know, too, what is meant by faith in the Lord Jesus Christ.'

With the coming of the text, Luther passes from the realm of *fear* into the realm of faith. It is like passing from the rigours of an arctic night into the sunshine of a summer day; it is like passing from a crowded city slum into the fields where the daffodils dance and the linnets sing; it is like passing into a new world; it is like *entering Paradise!*

VIII

Yes, it is like *entering Paradise!* The expression is his, not mine. 'Before those words broke upon my mind,' he says, 'I hated God and was angry with Him because, not content with frightening us sinners by the law and by the miseries of life, he still further increased our torture by the gospel. But when, by the Spirit of God, I understood these words—

"The just shall live by faith!"

"The just shall live by faith!"

—then I felt born again like a new man; I entered through the open doors into *the very Paradise of God!'*

'Henceforward,' he says again, 'I saw the beloved and holy Scriptures with other eyes. The words that I had previously detested, I began from that hour to value and to love as the sweetest and most consoling words in the Bible. In very truth, this text was to me *the true gate of Paradise!'*

'An open door into the very Paradise of God!'

'This text was to me the true gate of Paradise!'

And they who enter into the City of God by that gate will go no more out for ever.

III

SIR JOHN FRANKLIN'S TEXT

I

A HEAP of books and bones—and that was all!
One after another, no fewer than forty intrepid
navigators had invaded the awful solitudes of the
Arctic seas in quest of some trace of Sir John
Franklin and his gallant men; and *this* was the
tardy and the meagre reward of those long, long
years of search! On the snow-bound coast of a
large but inhospitable island, Sir Francis McClintock
discovered an overturned and dilapidated boat.
Underneath it, together with a few guns and
watches, they found a collection of bones and of
books. The men had been more than ten years
dead. Sir John Franklin, it was known, from
documents found elsewhere, had died upon his ship.
His last moments were cheered by the knowledge,
which came to him just in time, that the expedition
had been successful, and that the long-dreamed-of
North-West-Passage had been proved to be a fact.
The other members of the expedition, more than a
hundred and twenty men, had made an attempt to
save their lives by an overland dash. The natives
had seen that shadowy and wavering line of wan-
derers. They were very thin, the Eskimos said,

and could with difficulty stagger along. With every
mile, some fell out and lay down in the snow to die.
Others, according to an old native woman who met
them, seemed to die upon their feet, and they only
fell because death had already overtaken them. But,
of all the members of the Franklin expedition, these
were the first whose bones were actually found.
And, with the bones, some books! It was the *bones*
that principally interested their discoverers: it is
the *books* that must principally interest us. For
some of these saturated and frozen volumes were
once the personal property of Sir John Franklin.
Do they not still bear his name? One of them is a
battered copy of Dr. John Todd's *Student's Manual.*
Sir John has turned down a leaf in order to mark
a passage that appears on almost the last page of the
book.

'"Are you not afraid to die?"'

'No!'

'No! Why does the uncertainty of another state
give you no concern?'

'Because God has said to me: *"Fear not; when
thou passest through the waters, I will be with thee;
and through the rivers, they shall not overflow thee!"'*

There, as though his frozen finger pointed to it,
stands Sir John Franklin's text.

II

'The waters! The waters!'
'The beckoning, challenging waters!'

'When thou passest through the waters!'

From his earliest boyhood the waters had called
him. He lived in an inland town : his parents de-
signed him for the church : he was to be a bishop,
so they said! But a holiday at the seaside makes
all the difference. He walks up and down the sands
looking out on the infinite expanse of water. He
climbs the broken cliffs, and shading his eyes with his
hand, watches the great ships vanish over the distant skyline. The unseen taunts his imagination :
it alters the whole course of his life. The sight of
the sea awakens a tempest of strange passions in
his soul. Distant voices call him and distant fingers
beckon. To be a sailor! To be the first that ever
burst into some silent sea! His fancy catches fire
at the very thought of it!

The waters! The waters!

The call of the waters!

'When thou passest through the waters!'

He yields himself to the impulse that he scarcely
has the power to resist. He gives himself to the
waters, and he learns the business of seamanship
from the most distinguished masters of all time.
With Matthew Flinders, the most audacious and
the most unfortunate of our Australian explorers,
he circumnavigates this great continent; whilst at
Copenhagen and Trafalgar he fights beneath 'the
greatest sailor since the world began.' He makes
friends, too, with men who have sailed with Cap-
tain Cook, from one of whom, Sir Joseph Banks, he

catches the inspiration that sends him cruising into
Arctic seas. But whether in peaceful exploration or
amidst the excitements of war, whether in the
sunny South or in the frigid and desolate North,
he is for ever listening to the voices of the waters.
He knows what the wild waves are saying. They
are calling him to come. And he obeys. For in his
heart he cherishes a wonderful secret. The unknown waters are not as lonely as they seem.

The shining tropical waters!

The frozen polar waters!

The unseen, unsailed waters!

*'When thou passest through the waters, I will
be with thee!'*

The delightful eyes of Franklin behold a sea of
significance in that.

III

A dauntless explorer and a brilliant discoverer
was Franklin, but by far the most fruitful discovery of his adventurous life was made in 1820.
He was then in his thirty-fifth year, and was un-
dergoing his first experience of the ice-bound North.
He was in charge of the overland section of the
expedition, and was compelled to winter at Fort
Enterprise, a desolate spot half way between the
Great Bear Lake and the Great Slave Lake. It
was a weird experience—so cold, so dark, so still!
In a letter to his sister, written from this out-
landish solitude, he speaks of the astonishing way

in which, during the intense Arctic silence, his
Bible breaks with new beauty upon him. It is not
the same book. The surprises grow in novelty and
wonder every day. Everything in the sacred volume, and especially the central story—the story
of redeeming love—acquires a new glory in his en-
raptured eyes. In this hushed wilderness of snow
and ice, he has abundant time for thought. Such
serious reflection, he says, must soon convince a
sinner of his guilt, of his inability to do anything
to save himself, and of his urgent need of deliverance. 'If, under this conviction, he should
enquire, "*How, then, can I be saved?*" would it not
be joy unspeakable for him to find that the gospel
points out the way? Christ who died for the salvation of sinners is *the Way, the Truth and the
Life. Whoso cometh unto Him* in full purpose of
heart *shall in no wise be cast out.* Can anything
be more cheering than these assurances, or better
calculated to fill the mind with heavenly impressions and lift up the heart in grateful adoration to
God?'

'*How, then, can I be saved?*'

'*I am the Way, the Truth, and the Life. Him
that cometh unto Me I will in no wise cast out.*'

He has heard the call of the waters; and on his
very first venture into the cold and silent North,
he has discovered *this!* He has found, not only
a Saviour, but a Friend. He has received the
assurance, on whatever seas he sails, of a divine

Presence, a sacred Comradeship; and, to the end of his life, he never ceased to prize it.

IV

The saint is never cast in a mould: no two are alike. On my desk at this moment lie two books side by side. One is the *Life of Sir John Franklin*, the other is Brother Lawrence's *Practice of the Presence of God*. Can any greater contrast be imagined? Here are two types of saintliness: neither appears to have anything in common with the other. For one man is a monk: the other is a mariner. The one is a recluse, moving among the cells and cloisters of a Carmelite Monastery: the other travels over all the continents and sails into all the seas. The one is essentially an ascetic: the other is essentially a man of the world. The one is pale and thin and sad: the other is bluff and bronzed and jolly. And yet I am impressed at this moment, not by the contrast, but by the similitude. Let us look for a moment beneath the trappings alike of the *monk* and of the *mariner;* and, in each case, let us search the soul of the *man.*

'I have quitted all forms of devotion,' says Brother Lawrence, 'but those to which my state obliges me. And I make it my business only to persevere in *His holy presence.* I am assured beyond all doubt that my soul has been with God above these thirty years. Were I a preacher, I should above all other things preach the practice of *the presence of God;* and, were I a director, I should advise all the world to it, so necessary do I think it, and so easy, too. I cannot imagine how religious persons can live satisfied without the practice of *the presecne of God* while I am with Him I fear nothing, but the least turning from Him is insupportable.'

Now, had I not revealed the source of these words, nobody could have told whether I had copied them from the conversations of the monk or from the journal of the mariner. They fell from the lips of Brother Lawrence; but they might just as as easily have occurred in the correspondence of Franklin. For it was the joy of Franklin's life, and the comfort of his death, that he could never be alone. *'When thou passest through the waters,'* the promise said, *'I will be with thee';* and he believed it. The thought runs through all his farewell letters. His leave-taking reminds one of Enoch Arden's.

> Keep everything shipshape, for I must go!
> And fear no more for me; or, if you fear,
> Cast all your cares on God; that anchor holds!
> Is He not yonder in those uttermost
> Parts of the morning? If I flee to these,
> Can I go from Him? And the sea is His,
> The sea is His; He made it!

On the night before the ships sailed on that last fatal voyage, he expressed his confidence in the

divine care; in all the blunt sailor-sermons that
he preached to his officers and men amidst the ice,
the same thought was always uppermost; and the
book, with the leaf turned down at the text, shows
that his confidence held out to the last

The white, white waters!

The cruel and pitiless waters!

The all-engulfing waters!

*'When thou passest through the waters, I will
be with thee!'*

In life, and in death, that anchor held!

V

Yes, the anchor held; but the strain upon it was
at times terrific. What test, for example, can be
more severe than the test of slow starvation? And,
more than once, Franklin's faith was subjected to
that terrible ordeal. The ragamuffins in the London
streets used to call Franklin 'the man who ate his
own boots,' and he lived to laugh with them at the
joke; but it was grim enough experience at the
time. The horror of it invaded his sleep for years
afterwards. They are out amidst the snowy vast-
nesses of the interior when the food fails. They
divide into two parties: Franklin leads the stronger
men in an attempt to find provisions, whilst Dr.
Richardson remains to nurse the more exhausted
members of the expedition. The foraging party
has no success; and all are reduced to skeletons.

Whilst Franklin and his companions are resting, Dr. Richardson and a seaman of his party come spectrally upon them. They are the only survivors of the group left at the camp! All are soon too feeble to move. In their extremity a herd of reindeer trot by; but the men are too exhausted to fire! Franklin remembers the promise, and, with thin and wavering voice, leads the party in prayer. And this is the next entry in his journal:—

'Nov. 7, 1821. Praise be to the Lord! We were this day rejoiced at noon by the appearance of Indians with supplies!'

'Old Franklin,' so wrote a midshipman to his friends at home, 'old Franklin is an exceedingly good old chap and very clever. We are all delighted with him. He is quite a bishop. We have church morning and evening on Sundays, the evening service in the cabin to allow of the attendance of the watch that could not be present in the forenoon. We all go both times. The men say they would rather have him than half the parsons in England.'

For, after all, there is no eloquence like the eloquence of conviction, and out of the depths of a great and wonderful experience Sir John addressed his men.

The waters!

The wide, wide waters!

The waves on which the Lord was always walking!

'When thou passest through the waters, I will be with thee!'

The cable often quivered, but the anchor held!

VI

'When thou passest through the waters, I will be with thee!'

Franklin found the Lord walking on all the waters. Lying on my desk is an ancient map of the world which an old pilot showed to Henry the Seventh in the year 1500. One or two continents are missing, but there are ample compensations! For, all over the unexplored territory, I find written: 'Here be dragons!' 'Here be demons!' 'Here be sirens!' 'Here be savages that worship devils!' and so on. But, on *his* map of the world, Franklin wrote across all the unknown lands and all the un-charted seas, *'Here is God!' 'When thou passest through the waters, I will be with thee!'* And he always found Him there.

'When thou passest through the waters, I will be with thee!'

Who shall doubt that when, at last, he set out upon that strange voyage on unknown seas which, sooner or later, we must all undertake, he still found the promise true? When Lord Tennyson was asked to write an inscription for the monument in Westminster Abbey, he composed the lines that are recognised as one of the real adornments of the Abbey:—

Not here! the White North hath thy bones, and thou,
    Heroic Sailor Soul!
Art passing on thy happier voyage now
    Towards no earthly Pole!

'*Passing!*'

'*Passing on thy happier voyage!*'

'*When thou passest . . . I will be with thee!*'

Who, I say, can doubt the Presence Divine on
those uncharted waters?

When, in 1875, at the age of eighty-three, Lady
Franklin passed away, Dean Stanley added a post-
script to Lord Tennyson's inscription. It declared
that the monument in the Abbey was '*Erected by
his widow, who, after long waiting and sending
many in search of him, herself departed to seek and
to find him in the realms of light.*'

Thus, He who is with each of His voyagers when
they sail upon strange waters brings them safely
home and safely together; and, in the bliss of
arrival and reunion, the fierce storms and the long
separations are alike forgotten.

IV

THOMAS BOSTON'S TEXT

I

A WINDING, zig-zag path ascends the steep green
hill beside the stream; and an elderly man, somewhat bent, and leaning heavily upon his stick, is
toiling slowly and painfully up the slope. He pauses,
partly to take breath and partly that he may turn
and survey the exquisite panorama of emerald woodland and sparkling stream. But the grandeur of the
silent hills, the perfume of the tossing hyacinths, the
chirping of the grasshoppers at his feet, and the
haunting laughter of the silvery stream below, all
fail to gladden him to-day. The beauteous landscape of leafy wold and laughing water is bathed in
radiant sunshine; yet for him the skies are gray and
the earth is wrapped in gloom. His countenance is
sad and pensive, for he is conjuring up the memories
of happier days. He is thinking of those whom
he has loved long since and lost awhile. He knows
that this must be his final visit to the enchanting
valley that has inspired some of his tenderest poetry.
For this is William Wordsworth. He has written
'Yarrow Unvisited,' 'Yarrow Visited,' and 'Yarrow
Revisited,' and now he has come to take a last lingering farewell of the lovely place. He thinks of

those in whose sweet society he first explored its
flowery fields and forest paths—thinks especially of
two. He thinks of Dorothy, his sister, with whom
he walked, hand in hand, along these soft and
grassy banks in the days of long ago. He owes
everything to Dorothy. It was Dorothy who made
him a poet. And now Dorothy is ill, so ill that she
can never really recover! Then, turning to the east,
he shades his eyes with his hand and looks wistfully
towards Abbotsford. For it was Sir Walter Scott
who first welcomed him to this delightful spot.
Only a few months ago they rambled through these
woodland paths together. And now Scott is dead!
He who was the life and soul of this romantic
countryside will climb its hills and ford its streams
no more! To Wordsworth, the rugged slopes and
the wooded valleys, the waving grasses and the
murmuring torrent, are all lamenting the loss of one
who loved them each so well. There are few things
more affecting than to find the old familiar places,
but to miss the old familiar faces. Wordsworth
passes sadly over the crest of the hill to revisit the
Yarrow vale no more. Scott is dead! This was
in 1832.

II

We will remain in this same delightful neigh-
bourhood, but we will go back exactly a hundred
years. Scott died in 1832. In 1732 an old minister
whose manse stood just at the foot of yonder hill,

lay dying. He has come to within a few days of
his triumphant departure. But, although death is
stamped upon his face, and it is known that he
will never leave his bed again, it is announced that
he will preach on Sunday, morning and evening,
as usual! He orders his bed to be drawn up to
the window, and prepares to address his people for
the last time. Sunday comes From all the farms
and homesteads of that Selkirkshire countryside,
ploughmen and shepherds, accompanied by their
wives and children, set out early in the morning to
hear their old minister's last words. From all round
the slopes of Ettrick Pen, from the distant foothills
of Broad Law, from the lovely shores of St. Mary's
Lake, from all down the valleys of the Ettrick and
the Yarrow, little groups of men and women make
their way with heavy footsteps to the manse. The
church at the foot of the knoll, the church with its
quaint old tower, the church in which he has ministered for five and twenty years, is closed to-day.
The dying man has turned his deathbed into a
pulpit, and the whole countryside has gathered to
listen to his last message. The eager multitude
stretches far beyond the reach of his thin and
wavering voice. But those who cannot hear can
at least see his pale, wan face, and note the fire in
his eye that even death is impotent to quench. As
he sits, propped up by pillows, pleading with his
people for the last time, the mountain breezes play
with his thin, silvery hair. He exhausts the last

atom of his failing strength as he pours out his
soul in affectionate admonition and passionate entreaty. His voice falters; the watchers round the
bed gently remove the pillows that support him, and
he lies prostrate, breathing heavily; the window is
closed, and the great black crowd, breaking up into
little groups again, melts sadly and silently away.
In a few days it is tearfully whispered in every
cottage that Thomas Boston is dead. So ended one
of the most fruitful and memorable ministries that
even Scotland has enjoyed. In 1732, as in 1832,
there was sorrow in all that countryside. In 1732,
as in 1832, the Valley of the Yarrow was a vale of
tears.

III

Whenever I am inclined to pessimism, or am
tempted to suppose that modern conditions preclude
the possibility of a rich and fruitful ministry, I
reflect on the conditions that beset poor Thomas
Boston. On the self-same day that witnessed the
union under one crown of the English and Scottish
realms, on May Day, 1707, Boston settled at Ettrick. The church had but few members, and even
these were of such a type that their behaviour was
a reproach to the sanctuary. The poor minister,
whose heart was still tender at leaving his first
people, was horrified to find that his new parishioners could scarcely speak without profanity, and were
addicted to lives of the grossest immorality. Their

sins, moreover, were absolutely shameless. They were 'smart and of an uncommon assurance, self-conceited and censorious to a pitch.' Even when they came to church, their conduct was disorderly and indecent to the last degree. Many of them loitered about the churchyard, arguing and brawling whilst worship was proceeding; and elders had to be told off to keep order both inside and outside of the building. It was three years before Mr. Boston would allow the Lord's Supper to be observed among them. 'I have been much discouraged with respect to my parish a long time,' he says in his *Memoirs,* 'and have had little hand or heart for my work.' For twenty-five years, however, he ministered incessantly to this people. He visited them all in their homes; pleaded with them each in secret; invited the heads of the household to the manse, and taught them how to conduct family worship. After three years he was sufficiently assured of the sincerity of a handful of his people to admit them to the Lord's Table. Five years later, he is delighted at finding that he has a hundred and fifty devout communicants. Later still, he witnesses the most surprising spectacle in this same valley. People come in streams from far and near to be present at the Communion Service at Ettrick. 'It often reminded him of the Jewish Pilgrims in Old Testament times ascending in companies to Jerusalem to keep their Passover.' When the sacred season came round he had to call in other ministers to help him dispense the mystic symbols. The wilderness had become a fruitful field. The Ettrick manse was every week the resort of eager penitents, who, beholding with amazement the transformation in so many lives around them, were anxious to catch the holy contagion. In every house, family worship sanctified the opening and sweetened the close of each succeeding day. And the old church under the hill was, to hundreds and hundreds of people, the dearest spot that eyes had ever seen.

IV

Did I say that, when they withdrew the bed from the window, and the dying minister turned his face to the wall, his memorable ministry ended? If so, it was a slip of the pen, and an unpardonable slip at that. It is every man's duty to provide himself with some honest work that he may do when he is lying in his grave. Boston did; for, when the ministry of his lips ended, the ministry of his pen began. For years after his death, Thomas Boston's books were the most popular and most powerful works in Scotland; and, by means of them, the fragrance that had for so long filled the Ettrick Valley was wafted far and wide. Whilst Thomas Boston was lying in his grave, his influence was growing by leaps and bounds. Speaking of one of the books, *The Fourfold State,* Dr. Andrew Thomson, in his Introduction to Boston's *Life and Times,* says that within a quarter of a century

after its publication, it had found its way and was
eagerly read and pondered, over the Scottish Low-
lands. 'From St. Abb's Head to the remotest point
in Galloway it was to be seen side by side with the
Bible and Bunyan on the shelf in every peasant's
cottage. The shepherd bore it with him, folded in
his plaid, up among the silent hills; the ploughman
in the valleys refreshed his spirit with it, as with
heavenly manna, after his long day of toil. The
influence, which began with the humble classes,
ascended like a fragrance into the mansions of the
Lowland laird and the Border chief, and carried
with it a new and hallowed joy.' And, on the
authority of one who lived nearer to Boston's time,
he says that for three generations this book was
the instrument of more numerous conversions and
more extensive spiritual quickening than any other
volume he could name. And has not Dr. Thomas
McCrie, one of the greatest authorities on Scottish
life and literature, who was himself born in the same
little Border town in which Boston first saw the
light, spoken of *The Fourfold State* as a book that
has contributed more than any other work to mould
the religious sentiments of the Scottish people?

V

Now, where was this lamp lit, and by what flame
was it kindled? From infancy Boston was taught
to take religion seriously. Had not his father endured imprisonment for conscience' sake, and had

not Thomas, as a little boy, sat with him in his cell
to help relieve his loneliness? But when the lad
was twelve years of age, the Rev. Henry Erskine,
a name that must always hold a charm to Scottish
folk, came into the Border Country and began to
preach. From every direction people flocked to
hear him. John Boston went, taking little Thomas
with him. They were deeply moved, and went
again. Then, one never-to-be-forgotten day, Mr.
Erskine cried out, '*Behold the Lamb of God that
taketh away the sin of the world! Behold the Lamb
of God that taketh away the sin of the world!*'
What mountainous words!

The Lamb! . . . . The Sin!
God! . . . . The World!
The Lamb of God!
The Sin of the World!
The Lamb that taketh away the Sin!

'By this,' says Boston, 'I judge God spake to me.
I know I was touched to the quick at the first hearing, wherein I was like one amazed with some new
and strange thing. Sure I am I was in good
earnest concerned for a saving interest in Jesus
Christ. My soul went out after Him, and the place
of His feet was glorious in mine eyes.'

VI

The day on which that stupendous pronouncement
was first made was the day on which the slow
evolution of prophecy reached its culmination and

its climax. In the gray dawn of history a youth had climbed Mount Moriah, walking by his father's side, asking as he walked one pertinent and tragic question: 'My father, behold the fire and the wood, but where is the lamb for the burnt offering?'

'Where is the Lamb?'

'Where is the Lamb?'

The question, once started, echoed down the ages from generation to generation. For twenty centuries it haunted the hearts of men. And then, one day, the people were assembling at Jerusalem for the Passover, the Feast of the Lamb that was Slain. The thought of sacrifice, and especially of the sacrifice of the Lamb, was in every mind. And, as they flocked together to listen to the preaching of a strange, prophetic figure from the desert, the speaker caught sight of a Face in the crowd, a Face such as earth had never seen before. And, forsaking the beaten track of his discourse, he cried out: *'Behold the Lamb of God that taketh away the sin of the world!'* The riddle of the ages was read at last!

'Behold the Lamb!'

'Behold the Lamb!'

'I once stood in the valley of the Rees River at the head of Lake Wakatipu,' says Dr. Rutherford Waddell, 'and looked up at the great glacier heights of Mount Earnslaw. Far away up across the mountain brow innumerable rills and streams of water were pouring like silver bars down towards the

pine forests that climb the mountain-side. Across
vast widths of snow and ice they converged their
multitudinous rills; and by the time they had
reached the forests they had united their streams
into one great torrent. This comes tumbling down,
forming the beautiful Lennox Waterfall, and then,
leaping forth, it hurries away hence to the plain,
singing the song of liberty and life. So all the
diverging streams of ancient thought and Hebrew
prophecy meet in one great announcement. The
long evolution of the ages finds its culmination at
last in a living Person: *"Behold the Lamb of God
that taketh away the sin of the world!"'* Boston
heard Erskine repeat that stupendous declaration
in a little Border town, and all his heart stood up
to greet its deep and awful significance.

VII

But what is that profound significance? The
Lamb! The Lamb of God! The Lamb that taketh
away the Sin! What does it mean? The Lamb
stands for two things, two and no more. It is the
symbol of *Innocence,* and it is the symbol of *Suffering.* These two factors in human experience—
Innocence and Suffering—are united in the symbol-
ism of the lamb; and they are united in the eternal
scheme of things. For the dark tragedy of human
guilt passes through two stages. There is the
preliminary stage: the stage in which *the guilt of
the Guilty is the torture of the Innocent*—the father

heartbroken at his daughter's shame; the mother weeping over the excesses of her dissolute boy. And there is the subsequent stage, the stage in which *the innocence of the Innocent is the torture of the Guilty*—Legree tormented by the lock of his mother's hair; Dombey racked in the day of his ruin by the fact that 'every loving blossom he had withered in his innocent daughter's heart was snowing down in ashes on him.' The first of these principles—the torture of the Innocent by the guilt of the Guilty—led to *Redemption.* The second of these principles—the torture of the Guilty by the innocence of the Innocent—leads to *Repentance.* The first led the Son of the Highest to become the Lamb of God; the second led to the transformation in the soul of Boston when the great revelation burst upon him.

VIII

The startling proclamation that had so captivated his own heart became the keynote of Boston's historic and epoch-making ministry. 'From the time of my settling here,' he says, 'the great thing I aimed at in my preaching was to impress the people with a sense of their need of Christ.' In his later years Boston became convinced that a good sermon ought to be frequently repeated. He himself preached one sermon again and again and again. Its text was: *'Behold the Lamb of God that taketh away the sin of the world!'* And when the people gathered that Sunday under the bedroom window to hear his dying message, he still urged them with many tears to fix their eyes and their affections upon the Lamb of God. When Boston's sun was setting in Scotland, Wesley's was rising in England. It was in those days that Charles Wesley sang:

> Happy, if with my latest breath
> I may but gasp His name;
> Preach Him to all, and cry in death,
> 'Behold, behold the Lamb!'

And whilst, in England, Charles Wesley coveted for himself so sublime an experience, Thomas Boston, in Scotland, actually tasted its felicity.

V

HUGH LATIMER'S TEXT

I

THERE is excitement in the streets of London!
Who is this upon whom the crowd is pressing as he
passes down the Strand? Women throw open the
windows and gaze admiringly out; shopkeepers rush
from behind their counters to join the throng as it
approaches; apprentices fling aside their tools and,
from every lane and alley, pour into the street;
waggoners rein in their horses and leave them for a
moment unattended; the taverns empty as the procession draws near them! Everybody is anxious
to catch a glimpse of this man's face; to hear, if
possible, the sound of his voice: or, better still, to
clasp his hand as he passes. For this is Hugh
Latimer; the terror of evil-doers; the idol of the
common people; and, to use the phraseology of a
chronicler of the period, 'the honestest man in
England.' By sheer force of character he has
raised himself from a ploughman's cottage to a
bishop's palace—an achievement that, in the sixteenth century, stands without precedent or parallel.
'My father was a yeoman,' he says, in the course
of a sermon preached before the King, 'my father
was a yeoman, and had no lands of his own; he

had a farm of three or four pounds a year at the
utmost, and hereupon he tilled so much as kept
half-a-dozen men. He had walk for a hundred
sheep; and my mother milked thirty kine. He
kept me at school, or else I had not been able to
have preached before the King's majesty now.'
Nor has his elevation spoiled him. He has borne
with him in his exaltations the spirit of the common
people. He feels as they feel; he thinks as they
think; he even speaks as they speak. It was said
of him, as of his Master, that the common people
heard him gladly. In cathedral pulpits and royal
chapels he speaks a dialect that the common people
can readily understand; he uses homely illustra-
tions gathered from the farm, the kitchen and the
counting-house; he studiously eschews the pedantries
of the schoolmen and the subtleties of the theologians. His sermons are, as Macaulay says, 'the
plain talk of a plain man, who sprang from the
body of the people, who sympathized strongly with
their wants and their feelings, and who boldly
uttered their opinions.' It was on account of the
fearless way in which stout-hearted old Hugh ex-
posed the misdeeds of men in ermine tippets and
gold collars that the Londoners cheered him as he
walked down the Strand to preach at Whitehall,
struggled for a touch of his gown, and bawled,
'Have at them, Father Latimer!' There he goes,
then, a man of sound sense, honest affection, earnest
purpose and sturdy speech; a man whose pale face,

stooping figure and emaciated frame show that it
has cost him something to struggle upwards from
the ploughshare to the palace; a man who looks for
all the world like some old Hebrew prophet trans-
planted incongruously into the prosaic life of London! He passes down the Strand with the people
surging fondly around him. He loves the people,
and is pleased with their confidence in him. His
heart is simple enough and human enough to find
the sweetest of all music in the plaudits that are
ringing in his ears. So much for London; we must
go to Oxford!

II

There is excitement in the streets of Oxford!
Who is this upon whom the crowd is pressing as
he passes down from the Mayor's house to the open
ground in front of Balliol College? Again, women
are leaning out of the windows; shopkeepers are
forsaking their counters; apprentices are throwing
aside their tools; and drivers are deserting their
horses that they may stare at him. It is Hugh
Latimer again! He is a little thinner than when
we saw him in London; for he has exchanged a
palace for a prison. The people still press upon
him and make progress difficult; but this time they
crowd around him that they may curse him!
It is the old story of 'Hosannah!' one day and
'Away with Him! Crucify Him!' the next. The
multitude is a fickle master. Since we saw him in

the Strand, the crown has passed from one head
to another; the court has changed its ways to
gratify the whims of its new mistress; the Government has swung round to match the moods of the
court, and the people, like sheep, have followed
their leaders.   They are prepared now to crown
the men whom before they would have crucified,
and to crucify the men whom they would then have
crowned   But Hugh Latimer and his companion
—for this time he is not alone—are not of the
same accommodating temper.   Hugh Latimer is
still 'the honestest man in England!' His conscience
is still his only monitor; his tongue is still free; his
soul is not for sale! And so—

> In Oxford town the faggots they piled,
> With furious haste and with curses wild,
> Round two brave men of our British breed,
> Who dared to stand true to their speech and deed;
> Round two brave men of that sturdy race,
> Who with tremorless souls the worst can face;
> Round two brave souls who could keep their tryst
> Through a pathway of fire to follow Christ.
> And the flames leaped up, but the blinding smoke
> Could not the soul of Hugh Latimer choke;
> For, said he, 'Brother Ridley, be of good cheer,
> A candle in England is lighted here,
> Which by grace of God shall never go out!'—
> And that speech in whispers was echoed about—
> Latimer's Light shall never go out,
> However the winds may blow it about
> Latimer's Light has come to stay
> Till the trump of a coming judgement day.

'Bishop Ridley,' so runs the record, 'first entered

the lists, dressed in his episcopal habit; and, soon after, Bishop Latimer, dressed, as usual, in his prison garb. Master Latimer now suffered the keeper to pull off his prison-garb and then he appeared in his shroud. Being ready, he fervently recommended his soul to God, and then he delivered himself to the executioner, saying to the Bishop of London these prophetical words: "We shall this day, my lord, light such a candle in England as shall never be extinguished!" '

But it is time that we went back forty years or so, to a time long before either of the processions that we have just witnessed took place. We must ascertain at what flame the light that kindled that candle was itself ignited.

III

Very early in the sixteenth century, England was visited by one of the greatest scholars of the Renaissance, Desiderius Erasmus. After being welcomed with open arms at the Universities, he returned to the Continent and engrossed himself in his learned researches. At Cambridge, however, he had made a profound and indelible impression on at least one of the scholars. Thomas Bilney, familiarly known as 'Little Bilney,' was feeling, in a vague and indefinite way, the emptiness of the religion that he had been taught. He felt that Erasmus possessed a secret that was hidden from English eyes, and he vowed that, whatever it might

cost him, he would purchase every line that came
from the great master's pen. In France, Erasmus
translated the New Testament into Latin. The in-
genuity and industry of Bilney soon secured for
him a copy of the book. As to its effect upon him,
he shall speak for himself. 'My soul was sick,' he
says, 'and I longed for peace, but nowhere could
I find it. I went to the priests, and they appointed
me penances and pilgrimages; yet, by these things
my poor sick soul was nothing profited. But at
last I heard of Jesus. It was then, when first the
New Testament was set forth by Erasmus, that
the light came. I bought the book, being drawn
thereto rather by the Latin than by the Word of
God, for at that time I knew not what the Word of
God meant. And, on the first reading of it, as I
well remember, I chanced upon these words, *"This
is a faithful saying, and worthy of all acceptation,
that Christ Jesus came into the world to save sinners, of whom I am chief."* That one sentence,
through God's inward working, did so lift up my
poor bruised spirit that the very bones within me
leaped for joy and gladness. It was as if, after a
long, dark night, day had suddenly broke!' But
what has all this to do with Hugh Latimer?

IV

In those days Latimer was preaching at Cambridge, and all who heard him fell under the spell
of his transparent honesty and rugged eloquence.

Latimer was then the sturdy champion of the old
religion and the uncompromising foe of all who
were endeavouring to introduce the new learning.
Of all the friars, he was the most punctilious, the
most zealous, the most devoted. Bilney went to
hear him and fell in love with him at once. He
saw that the preacher was mistaken; that his eyes
had not been opened to the sublimities that had
flooded his own soul with gladness; but he recognised his sincerity, his earnestness and his resistless
power; and he longed to be the instrument of his
illumination. If only he could do for Latimer what
Aquila and Priscilla did for Apollos, and expound
unto him the way of God more perfectly! It became
the dream and desire of Bilney's life. 'O God,' he
cried, 'I am but "Little Bilney," and shall never do
any great thing for Thee; but give me the soul of
that man, Hugh Latimer, and what wonders *he*
shall do in Thy most holy Name!'

Where there's a will there's a way! One day,
as Latimer descends from the pulpit, he passes so
close to Bilney that his robes almost brush the
student's face. Like a flash, a sudden inspiration
leaps to Bilney's mind. 'Prithee, Father Latimer,'
he whispers, 'may I confess my soul to thee?' The
preacher beckons, and, into the quiet room adjoining, the student follows.

Of all the strange stories that heartbroken penitents have poured into the ears of Father-Confessors
since first the confessional was established, *that* was

the strangest! Bilney falls on his knees at Latimer's feet and allows his soul, pent up for so long, to utter itself freely at last. He tells of the aching hunger of his heart; he tells of the visit of Erasmus; he tells of the purchase of the book; and then he tells of the text. 'There it stood,' he says, the tears standing in his eyes, 'the very word I wanted. It seemed to be written in letters of light: *"This is a faithful saying, and worthy of all acceptation, that Christ Jesus came into the world to save sinners."* O Father Latimer,' he cries, the passion of his fervour increasing as the memory of his own experience rushes back upon him, 'I went to the priests and they pointed me to broken cisterns that held no water and only mocked my thirst! I bore the load of my sins until my soul was crushed beneath the burden! And then I saw that *"Christ Jesus came into the world to save sinners, of whom I am chief"*; and now, being justified by faith, I have peace with God through our Lord Jesus Christ!'

Latimer is taken by storm. He is completely overwhelmed. He, too, knows the aching dissatisfaction that Bilney has described. He has experienced for years the same insatiable hunger, the same devouring thirst. To the astonishment of Bilney, Latimer rises and then kneels beside him. The Father-Confessor seeks guidance from his penitent! Bilney draws from his pocket the sacred volume that has brought such comfort and such rapture to his own soul. It falls open at the passage that Bilney has read to himself over and over and over again: *'This is a faithful saying, and worthy of all acceptation, that Christ Jesus came into the world to save sinners, of whom I am chief.'* The light that never was on sea or shore illumines the soul of Hugh Latimer, and Bilney sees that the passionate desire of his heart has been granted him. And from that hour Bilney and Latimer lived only that they might unfold to all kinds and conditions of men the unsearchable riches of Christ.

V

'This is a faithful saying!' That is the preacher's comfort. In the course of a recent tour through Western Australia, I was taken through the gold diggings. And, near Kanowna, I was shown the spot on which, years ago, there gathered one of the largest and most extraordinary congregations that ever assembled on this side of the world. It was whispered all over the diggings that an enormous nugget had been found and that Father Long, the local priest, had seen it and knew exactly where it was discovered. Morning, noon and night the young priest was pestered by eager gold-hunters for information; but to one and all his lips were sealed. At last he consented to announce publicly the exact locality of the wonderful find. At the hour fixed men came from far and near, some on horseback, some on camels, some in all kinds of

conveyances, and thousands on foot. It was the largest gathering of diggers in the history of the gold fields. At the appointed time Father Long appeared, surveyed the great sea of bronzed and bearded faces, and then announced that the 'Sacred Nugget' had been found in the Lake Gwynne country. In a moment the crowd had vanished! There was the wildest stampede for the territory to which the priest had pointed them. But as the days passed by, the disappointed seekers, in twos and threes, came dribbing wearily back. Not a glint of gold had been seen by any of them! And then the truth flashed upon them. The priest had been hoaxed! The 'Sacred Nugget' was a mass of common metal splashed with gold paint! Father Long took the matter bitterly to heart; he went to bed a broken and humiliated man; and, a few months later, disconsolate, he died! It was a great day in Hugh Latimer's life when he got among the *'faithful sayings,'* the sayings of which he was certain, the sayings that could never bring to any confiding hearer the heartbreak and disgust of disappointment.

VI

'It is worthy of all acceptation!' It is worthy! It is worthy of *your* acceptance, your Majesty, for this proclamation craves no patronage! It is worthy of *your* acceptance, your Excellency, your Grace, my Lords, Ladies and Gentlemen all, for the gospel asks no favours! It is worthy, worthy, worthy of

the acceptance of you *all!* Hugh Latimer stood before kings and courtiers, and declared that *'this is a faithful saying, and worthy of all acceptation, that Christ Jesus came into the world to save sinners.'* Never once did he forget the dignity of his message: it was faithful; it was worthy in its own right of the acceptance of the lordliest; and he himself staked his life upon it at the last!

VII

Dr. Archibald Alexander, of Princeton, was for sixty years a minister of Christ; and for forty of those years he was a Professor of Divinity. No man in America was more revered or beloved. He died on October 22, 1851 As he lay adying, he was heard by a friend to say, 'All my theology is reduced now to this narrow compass: *"This is a faithful saying, and worthy of all acceptation, that Christ Jesus came into the world to save sinners."'* In life and in death Hugh Latimer was of pretty much the same mind.

VI

JOHN BUNYAN'S TEXT

I

THERE is no doubt about John Bunyan's text. As a lover carves his lady's name on trees, signs it in mistake for his own, and mutters it in his sleep, so Bunyan inscribes everywhere the text that wrought his memorable deliverance. It crops up again and again in all his writings. The characters in his allegories, the dream-children of his fertile fancy, repeat it to each other as though it were a password, a talisman, a charm; he himself quotes it whenever the shadow of an opportunity presents itself; if it is not the text, it is at least the burden, of every sermon that he preaches. It sings itself through his autobiography like a repeating chorus, like an echoing refrain. By its radiance he extricates himself from every gloomy valley and from every darksome path. Its joyous companionship beguiles all his long and solitary tramps. It dispels for him the loneliness of his dreary cell. When no other visitor is permitted to approach the gaol, John Bunyan's text comes rushing to his memory as though on angel's wings. It sings to him its song of confidence and peace every morning; its music scatters

the gloom of every night. It is the friend of his
fireside; the companion of his solitude; the comrade
of his travels; the light of his darkness. It illumines
his path amidst the perplexities of life; it wipes
away his tears in the day of bitter sorrow; and it
smooths his pillow in the hour of death. When a
man habitually wears a diamond pin, you uncon-
sciously associate the thought of his face with the
thought of the gem that scintillates beneath it. In
the same way, nobody can have become in the slightest degree familiar with John Bunyan without
habitually associating the thought of his honest and
rugged personality with the thought of the text that
he made so peculiarly his own.

II

On the opening pages of *Pilgrim's Progress* we
come upon the principal character, all clothed in
rags, a heavy burden upon his back, greatly distressed in mind, walking in the fields and crying,
'What must I do to be saved?'

'Do you see yonder shining light?' asks Evangelist.

'I think I do,' replied the wretched man.

'Keep that light in your eye and go up directly
thereto; so shalt thou see a gate, at which, when
thou knockest, it shall be told thee what thou shalt
do!'

The man comes in due course to the gate and
knocks many times, saying:

May I now enter here? Will he within
Open to sorry me, though I have been
An undeserving rebel? Then shall I
Not fail to sing his lasting praise on high.

'I am willing with all my heart,' replies Good-
Will, the keeper of the gate, 'we make no objec-
tions against any. Notwithstanding all that they
have done before they come hither, they are *in no
wise cast out!*'

So Christian enters in at the gate and sets out on
pilgrimage. And there, at the very beginning of his
new life, stands the first vague but unmistakeable
suggestion of John Bunyan's text.

'In no wise cast out!'

'In no wise cast out!'

*'Him that cometh to Me, I will in no wise cast
out!'*

There, over the portal of the pilgrim path, stands
the text that gave John Bunyan to the world.

III

It stands over the very portal of his pilgrim's
path for the simple reason that it stands at the very
beginning of his own religious experience. Let us
turn from his allegory to his autobiography.

'In no wise cast out!' he exclaims, 'Oh, the comfort that I found in that word!'

'In no wise cast out!'

'In no wise cast out!'

We all know the story of the wretchedness which

that great word dispelled. It is one of the most moving records, one of the most pathetic plaints, in the language. Bunyan felt that he was a blot upon the face of the universe. He envied the toads in the grass by the side of the road, and the crows that cawed in the ploughed lands by which he passed. They, he thought, could never know such misery as that which bowed *him* down. 'I walked,' he says, in a passage that Macaulay felt to be specially eloquent and notable, 'I walked to a neighbouring town, and sat down upon a settle in the street, and fell into a very deep pause about the most fearful state my sin had brought me to; and, after long musing, I lifted up my head; but methought I saw as if the sun that shineth in the heavens did grudge to give me light; and as if the very stones in the street, and tiles upon the houses, did band themselves against me. Methought that they all combined together to banish me out of the world. I was abhorred of them, and unfit to dwell among them, because I had sinned against the Saviour. Oh, how happy now was every creature over me, for they stood fast and kept their station. But I was gone and lost!'

'*Gone and lost!*'

'*Gone and lost!*'

It was whilst he was thus lamenting his hopeless condition that the light broke. 'This scripture,' he says, 'did most sweetly visit my soul: "*and him that cometh to Me, I will in no wise cast out.*" O,

what did I now see in that blessed sixth of John!
O, the comfort that I had from this word!'

'In no wise cast out!'

'In no wise cast out!'

*'Him that cometh to Me, I will in no wise cast
out!'*

What was it that he saw in 'that blessed sixth
of John'? What was the comfort that he found
so lavishly stored there? The matter is worth in-
vestigating.

IV

In his pitiful distress, there broke upon the soul
of John Bunyan a vision of the infinite *approachability* of Jesus. That is one of the essentials of
the faith. It was for no other purpose that the
Saviour of men left the earth and enshrined Himself in invisibility. 'Suppose,' says Henry Drum-
mond, 'suppose He had not gone away; suppose He
were here now. Suppose He were still in the Holy
Land, at Jerusalem. Every ship that started for
the East would be crowded with Christian pilgrims.
Every train flying through Europe would be
thronged with people going to see Jesus. Every
mail-bag would be full of letters from those in
difficulty and trial. Suppose you are in one of those
ships. The port, when you arrive after the long
voyage, is blocked with vessels of every flag. With
much difficulty you land, and join one of the long
trains starting for Jerusalem. Far as the eye can

reach, the caravans move over the desert in an endless stream. As you approach the Holy City you see a dark, seething mass stretching for leagues and leagues between you and its glittering spires. You have come to see Jesus; but you will never see Him.' You are crowded out. Jesus resolved that this should never be. 'It is expedient for you,' he said, 'that I go away.' He went away in order to make Himself approachable! John Bunyan saw to his delight that it is possible for the most unworthy to go direct to the fountain of grace.

'Him that *cometh to Me!'*

'Him that *cometh to Me!'*

'Him that *cometh to Me,* I will in no wise cast out!'

John Bunyan's text was a revelation to him of the *approachability* of Jesus.

V

In his pitiful distress there broke upon the soul of John Bunyan a vision of the infinite *catholicity* of Jesus. Therein lay for him the beauty of the text. In the darkest hours of his wretchedness he never had any doubt as to the readiness of the Saviour to welcome to His grace certain fortunate persons. Holy Master Gifford, for example, and the poor women whom he overheard discussing the things of the kingdom of God as they sat in the sun beside their doors, and the members of the little church at Bedford; concerning the salvation of these

people Bunyan was as clear as clear could be. But
from such felicity he was himself rigidly excluded.
'About this time,' he says, 'the state of happiness
of these poor people at Bedford was thus, in a kind
of a vision, presented to me. I saw as if they were
on the sunny side of some high mountain, there
refreshing themselves with the pleasant beams of
the sun, while I was shivering and shrinking in
the cold, afflicted with frost, snow, and dark clouds.
Methought also, betwixt me and them, I saw a wall
that did compass about this mountain. Now through
this wall my soul did greatly desire to pass; concluding that, if I could, I would there also comfort
myself with the heat of their sun ' But he could
find no way through or round or over the wall.
Then came the discovery of the text. 'This scripture did most sweetly visit my soul; *"and him that
cometh to me, I will in no wise cast out."* Oh! the
comfort that I had from his word, *in no wise!* As
who should say, *"By no means,* for nothing whatever he hath done." But Satan would greatly labour to pull this promise from me, telling me that
Christ did not mean me and such as me, but sinners
of another rank, that had not done as I had done.
But I would answer him again. "Satan, here is in
these words no such exception; but him that cometh,
him, any him; *him that cometh to Me I will in no
wise cast out."* '
'*Him that cometh!*'
'*Any him! Any him!*'

'Him that cometh I will in no wise cast out!'

Like the gate that swings open on hearing the magic 'sesame'; like the walls that fell at Jericho when the blast of the trumpets arose; the wall round Bunyan's mountain fell with a crash before that great and golden word. *'Him that cometh to Me I will in no wise cast out!'* The barriers had vanished! The way was open!

'Him that cometh!'

'Any him! Any him!'

'Him that cometh to Me I will in no wise cast out!' Here was a vision of the *catholicity* of Jesus!

VI

In his pitiful distress there broke upon the soul of John Bunyan a vision of the infinite *reliability* of Jesus. It was the deep, strong accent of certainty that ultimately captivated all his heart. Times without number, he had come with a great 'perhaps' trembling on his lips. 'Often,' he tells us, 'when I had been making to the promise, I have seen as if the Lord would refuse my soul for ever, I was often as if I had run upon the pikes, and as if the Lord had thrust at me to keep me from him, as with a flaming sword. Then would I think of Esther, who went to petition the king contrary to the law. I thought also of Benhadad's servants, who went with ropes under their heads to their enemies for mercy. The woman of Canaan, that would not be daunted, though called 'dog' by Christ; and the man that went to borrow bread at midnight, were also great encouragements to me.' But each was, after all, only the encouragement of a possibility, of a probability, of a 'perhaps.'

Perhaps! Perhaps! Perhaps!

In contrast with all this, the text spoke out its message bravely. *'Him that cometh to Me I will in no wise cast out!'*

'In no wise! In no wise! In no wise!'

'Oh! the comfort that I had from this word: *"in no wise!"* . . . If ever Satan and I did strive for any word of God in all my life, it was for this good word of Christ: he at one end and I at the other. Oh! what work we made! It was for this in John, I say, that we did so tug and strive; he pulled, and I pulled; but God be praised, I overcame him; I got sweetness from it!' He passed at a bound from the Mists of the Valley to the Sunlight of the Summit. He had left the shadowland of 'perhaps' for the luxurious sunshine of a glowing certainty. 'With joy,' he says, 'I told my wife: "Oh, now *I know, I know, I know!"* That was a good night to me; I have had but few better. Christ was a precious Christ to my soul that night; I could scarce lie in my bed for joy and grace and triumph!'

Perhaps! Perhaps! Perhaps!
In no wise! In no wise! In no wise!
I know! I know! I know!

Thus Bunyan found in the radiance that streamed

from 'that blessed sixth of John,' a revelation of
the *reliability* of Jesus!

VII

Those who have studied Butler's *Analogy of
Religion* will recall the story that, in the introductory
pages, Mr. Malleson tells of the illustrious author.
When Bishop Butler lay upon his deathbed, Mr.
Malleson says, an overwhelming sense of his own
sinfulness filled him with a terrible concern. His
chaplain bent over him and tried to comfort him.

'You know, sir,' said the chaplain, 'that Jesus
is a great Saviour!'

'Yes,' replied the terror-stricken bishop. 'I know
that He died to save. But how shall I know that
He died to save *me?*'

'My Lord,' answered the chaplain, 'it is written
that *him that cometh to Me I will in no wise cast
out!*'

'True!' exclaimed the dying man, 'I am surprised
that, though I have read that scripture a thousand
times over, I never felt its virtue until this moment.
Now I die happy!'

And he did.

So, too, pillowing his head upon the selfsame
words, did Bunyan. 'His end,' says Froude, 'was
characteristic. It was brought on by exposure
when he was engaged in an act of charity. A
quarrel had broken out in a family at Reading with
which Bunyan had some acquaintance. A father

had taken some offence at his son, and threatened to disinherit him. Bunyan undertook a journey on horseback from Bedford to Reading in the hope of reconciling them. He succeeded, but at the cost of his life. Returning by way of London, he was overtaken on the road by a storm of rain, and was drenched before he could find shelter. The chill, falling on a constitution already weakened by illness, brought on fever. In ten days he was dead. His last words were: "Take me, for I come to Thee!" '

'*I come to Thee! I come to Thee!*'

'*Him that cometh to Me, I will in no wise cast out!*'

The words that had lit up the path of his pilgrimage illumined also the valley of the shadow of death! The words that opened to him the realms of grace opened also the gates of glory! The words that had welcomed him at the Wicket Gate welcomed him also to the Celestial City!

ƴ

VII

SIR WALTER SCOTT'S TEXT

I

IT was a very happy bridegroom and a very happy
bride that came to Lasswade Cottage early in 1798.
They had been married on Christmas Eve; and,
after a few days in Edinburgh, had come on to this
pretty little home on the banks of the Esk. Walter
Scott was twenty-six; not one of his books had
been written; no thought of fame had visited him;
he dreamed only the happiness that must be his in
the new life that he had so recently entered; whilst
she tells him that she is sure that he will rise in his
profession, become a judge, and die immensely
wealthy. Scott vows that he will make his riverside
home the sweetest spot beneath the stars. He takes
infinite pains in laying out the gardens and the
lawns. In the years that followed he never looked
upon any of his novels or biographies with greater
pride than that with which he surveyed the mystic
arch that he built with his own hands over the
gate that opened on the Edinburgh Road. In this
romantic home he spent some of the sunniest years
of his life; and, as Lockhart points out, it was
amongst these delicious solitudes that he produced
the works that laid the imperishable foundations of

all his fame. As you stroll about this pretty garden, and mark the diligence with which this young husband of ours has trained all his flowers and creepers, I would have you step out on to the lawn. And here, in the centre of the lawn, is a sundial. Our happy young bridegroom ordered it before his marriage, and it has been made to his design. See how carefully he has planted the creepers around it! And, according to custom, he has had a motto engraved upon the dial, a motto of his own selection. It consists of three Greek words: *'The Night Cometh!'* Scott was not morbid; he was a great human. But in the sunshine of life's morning he solemnly reminded himself that high noon is not a fixture. The brightest day wears away to evening at last. He horrified his bride-elect by arranging, before his marriage, for a place of burial. 'What an idea of yours,' she says in a letter written a few days before the wedding, 'what an idea of yours was that to mention where you wish to have your bones laid! If you were married I should think you were tired of me. A very pretty compliment before marriage! I hope sincerely that I shall not live to see that day. If you always have those cheerful thoughts, how very pleasant and gay you must be!' Poor, distressed little bride! But she soon found that her apprehensions were unfounded. Her lover was not as gloomy as she feared. He was reminding himself that the sunshine does not last for ever, it is true; but, just because the

sunshine does not last for ever, he was vowing that
he would make the most of it. *'The Night Cometh,'*
he wrote upon the sundial on the lawn. *'The night
cometh,'* therefore revel in the daylight whilst it
lasts! *'I must work the works of Him that sent
me whilst it is day; the night cometh when no man
can work.'*

II

The inscription on Sir Walter Scott's sundial
must have been suggested by the inscription on
Dr. Johnson's watch. Scott was a great admirer
of Johnson. In some respects there is a strong
resemblance between them. Sir Alfred Dale, Vice-
Chancellor of Liverpool University, recently referred to them as 'two of the most heroic and,
at the same time, most pathetic figures in the annals
of our literature.' Boswell's *Life of Johnson,* and
Lockhart's *Life of Scott* are, by common consent,
the two greatest biographies in the language. The
former was a new book, and was still the talk of
the town, in the days of Scott's courtship and marriage. And in that noble record of a noble life
Scott had read Boswell's account of the glimpse
that he once caught of the old doctor's watch. As
Dr. Johnson drew it from his pocket one day, Boswell noticed that on its face it bore a Greek inscription. The inscription consisted of the three
Greek words, *'The Night Cometh!'* It reminded
the doctor, whenever he consulted his watch, that

the daylight does not last for ever. *'Work whilst it is day,'* the watch seemed to say, *'for the night cometh when no man can work!'*

III

It is 1831. Scott is sixty now. It is thirty-three years since we saw him walking on the lawn at Lasswade Cottage with his bride. Then none of his books were written; now they are all complete Fame and honour are most richly his. His poor bride, however, had her wish. 'The burial of your bones!' she wrote, in pretty scorn, in the midst of her preparations for the wedding. 'I hope sincerely that I shall not live to see that day!' She did not. She has been five years dead. The brilliant sunshine of that early day has vanished; life is wearing towards its eventide *'The Night Cometh!'* Sir Walter is spending a day with old friends at Douglas. There is a sadness on his spirit that nothing can dispel; and once or twice, as he strides across old familiar landscapes, his companions catch the glint of tears upon his cheek. It has been agreed that there shall be no company but friends of old standing, and among these is Mr. Elliott Lockhart, whom Scott has not seen for many years. Since they last met, both men have been very ill. In the old days they followed the hounds together, and Lockhart was as handsome a specimen of a Border gentleman as ever cheered a hunting field. 'When they met now,' says the biographer, 'each saw his own case glassed in the other, and neither of their manly hearts could well contain itself as they embraced.' They part at night, Scott promising to call on his old friend in the course of his own homeward journey. 'But next morning, at breakfast, came a messenger to inform us that Mr. Lockhart, on returning to his own house, fell down in a fit, and that his life was despaired of. Immediately, although he had intended to remain two days, Sir Walter drew his host aside, and besought him to lend him horses as far as Lanark, for that he must set off with the least possible delay. He would listen to no persuasions. 'No, William,' he said, 'this is a sad warning. I must home to *work while it is called day; for the night cometh when no man can work.* I put that text many a year ago on my dialstone, but it often preached in vain.' It may have done. But anybody who surveys the long row of noble classics with which he has enriched our literature will feel that it must still more often have preached with remarkable effect.

IV

The Night!
The Night Cometh!

Was Sir Walter justified in reminding himself, amidst the dazzling sunshine of his wedding bliss, that the night cometh? Was old Dr. Johnson wise in confronting himself with that stern truth when-

ever he consulted his watch? Why not? Is the
night an ugly thing? I recall a very familiar incident in the life of Thomas Carlyle. One lovely
evening he and Leigh Hunt, the poet, strolled off
together amidst scenery that was full of rugged
grandeur and exquisite charm. Presently the stars
shone out, and added immeasurably to the glory
of the night. Both men gazed upon the heavens
for some moments in silence; and then the poet,
to whose soul they had been whispering of peace
and happiness and love, burst into the rapturous
exclamation, *'God the Beautiful!'* Immediately,
Carlyle, seeing only the dread majesty of heaven,
sprang to his feet and exclaimed, *'God the Terrible!'*
And both were right. The Night is Beautiful as
God is Beautiful! The Night is Terrible as God is
Terrible! Carlyle dreaded the Night as Scott
dreaded it, and as Johnson dreaded it. They all
three trembled lest the Night should fall before they
had finished the work which they had been appointed to do. 'The only happiness that a brave
man ever troubles himself much about,' I find
Carlyle saying, 'is happiness enough to get his work
done. Not "I can't eat!" but "I can't work!" *that*
is the burden of all wise complaining men. It is,
after all, the one unhappiness of a man that he
cannot work; that he cannot get his destiny as a
man fulfilled. Behold, the day is passing swiftly
away, our life is passing over; and *the night cometh
wherein no man can work!'* And who can forget

those sledge-hammer sentences with which he concludes his 'Everlasting Yea'? 'I say now to myself,
Produce! Produce! Were it but the pitifullest
infinitesimal fraction of a Product, produce it, in
God's name! 'Tis the utmost thou hast in thee;
out with it, then! Up; up! Whatsoever thy hand
findeth to do, do it with thy whole might! *Work
while it is called To-day; for the Night cometh,
wherein no man can work!*' And so twice, at least,
I find the Sage of Chelsea emphasising the text that
made the Wizard of the North.

'*The Night Cometh!*' says Dr. Johnson, and he
has the words inscribed upon the face of his watch.

'*The Night Cometh!*' says Sir Walter Scott, and
he has the words engraved on the sundial on the
lawn at Lasswade Cottage.

'*The Night Cometh!*' says Thomas Carlyle in
the pages of his first book, a book that was written
among the mosshags of Craigenputtock before the
world had even heard his name. '*Work while it is
called To-day; for the Night cometh, wherein no
man can work.*'

And these three—Johnson, Scott and Carlyle—
became three of the most prodigious workers·of all
history.

V

'*The Night Cometh!*' It came to Dr. Johnson,
the Night that he had dreaded for so long! 'The
infirmities of age,' says Macaulay, 'were creeping

fast upon him. That inevitable event of which he never thought without horror was brought near to him; and his whole life was darkened by the shadow of death.' It is not pleasant reading. Let us turn the page! And what is this? 'When at length the moment, dreaded through so many years, came close, the dark cloud passed away from Johnson's mind. His temper became unusually patient and gentle; he ceased to think with terror of death, and of that which lies beyond death; and he spoke much of the mercy of God and of the propitiation of Christ.' His faith triumphed over all his fears; he talked with rapture of the love of God; he pointed his friends to the Cross; and he confidently resigned his soul to his Saviour. *'The Night Cometh!'* he had said to himself with a shudder, over and over and over again. But when it came, that night was as tranquil as an infant's slumber and illumined by a million stars. The night that follows a great day's work well done is never a very terrible affair.

VI

'The Night Cometh!' It came to Sir Walter Scott, the Night of which the sundial had spoken so effectively and so long. We have all dwelt with lingering fondness on that closing scene. Here he is, at Abbotsford, surrounded by his grandchildren and his dogs. He is too feeble to rise, but, at his desire, they wheel him round the lawns in a bath-

chair. He strokes the hair of the children; pats the dogs on the heads; and pauses to admire his favourite roses.

'I have seen much in my time,' he whispers softly, 'but nothing like my ain house—give me one turn more!'

Exhausted by his ride, and by the tumult of emotions that it has awakened, the dying man is put to bed. Next morning he asks to be wheeled into the library. They place his chair against the central window that he may look down on the shining waters of the Tweed. He glances round upon the shelves containing his thousands of beloved books.

'Read to me!' he says to Lockhart.

'From what book shall I read?'

'Need you ask? There is but one!'

Lockhart takes down the Bible, and opens it at the fourteenth chapter of the Gospel of John.

'Let not your heart be troubled; ye believe in God, believe also in Me. In My Father's house are many mansions; if it were not so, I would have told you. I go to prepare a place for you . . .' And so on. The matchless cadences that have soothed and softened and sweetened a million deathbeds fall like a foretaste of the eternal harmonies upon the sick man's ear.

'This is a great comfort—a great comfort,' he murmurs.

He lingers for a while; but the atmosphere of

that conversation by the library window enfolds
him to the last. The Night comes; and with the
Night come weariness and restfulness and tired
hands gently folded.

VII

There is only one way of preparing for the night.
We must work! That is what Jesus said. *'We
must work while it is called To-day; the Night
cometh when no man can work!'* A good day's
work means a good night's rest. Johnson and Scott
and Carlyle had learned that secret, but it was from
Him that they learned it. And they became the men
that they were because they took His words and
engraved them on their watches and on their sundials. Yes, on their watches and on their sundials—
and on their hearts!

VIII

OLIVER CROMWELL'S TEXT

I

OLIVER CROMWELL ranks among the giants. Mr.
Frederic Harrison sets his name among the four
greatest that our nation has produced. Carlyle's
guffaw upon hearing this pretty piece of patronage
would have sounded like a thunderclap! Four, indeed! Carlyle would say that the other three would
look like a trio of travelling dwarfs grouped about a
colossus when they found themselves in the company of Oliver Cromwell. Carlyle can see nothing
in our history, nor in any other, more impressive
than the spectacle of this young farmer leaving his
fields in Huntingdonshire, putting his plough in the
shed, and setting out for London to hurl the king
from his throne, to dismiss the Parliament, and to
reconstitute the country on a new and better basis.
He was the one Strong Man; so much stronger than
all other men that he bent them to his will and
dominated the entire situation. Cromwell made
history wholesale. How? That is the question—
How? And what if, in our search for an answer
to that pertinent question, we discover that it was
by means of *a text?* Let us go into the matter.

II

My suspicions in this direction were first aroused
by reading a letter that Cromwell wrote to his
cousin, Mrs. St. John, before his public career had
begun. In this letter he refers to himself as 'a poor
creature.' 'I am sure,' he says, 'that I shall never
earn the least mite.' Here is strange language for
a man who, confident of his resistless strength, will
soon be overturning thrones and tossing crowns
and kingdoms hither and thither at his pleasure!
Is there nothing else in the letter that may help us
to elucidate the mystery? There is! He goes on
to tell his cousin that, after all, he does not entirely
despair of himself. Just one ray of hope has shone
upon him, one star has illumined the blackness of
his sky. *'One beam in a dark place,'* he says, *'hath
much refreshment in it!'* He does not tell his cousin
what that ray of hope is; he does not name that
solitary star; he does not go into particulars as to
that 'one beam in a dark place.' But we, for our
part, must prosecute our investigations until we have
discovered it.

III

It is sometimes best to start at the end of a
thing and to work backwards to the beginning.
We will adopt that plan in this instance. One who
was present at the closing scene has graphically
described it for us. 'At Hampton Court,' he says,

'being sick nigh unto death, and in his bed-chamber,
Cromwell called for his Bible and desired an hon-
ourable and godly person to read unto him
that passage in the fourth of Philippians which
saith, *"I can do all things through Christ that
strengtheneth me."* Which read, he observed, "This
scripture did once save my life, when my eldest
son, poor Robert, died, which went as a dagger to
my heart, indeed it did!" '

This does not tell us much; but it sets our feet
in the path that may lead to more. And at any
rate it makes clear to us what that 'one beam' was
that so often had much refreshment in it. *'I can
do all things through Christ that strengtheneth me.'*

IV

Groping our way back across the years by the
aid of the hint given us in those dying words, we
come upon that dark and tragic day, nineteen years
earlier, when the 'son of good promise' died. Un-
fortunately, the exact circumstances attending the
death of the young man have never been recorded.
Even the date is shrouded in mystery. Nobody
knows in which battle he fell. Perhaps the father
was too full of grief and bitterness to write for us
that sad and tragic tale. All that we know is what
he told us on his deathbed. He says that 'it went
like a dagger to my heart, indeed it did'; and he
says that it brought to his aid the text—the 'one
beam in a dark place'—that saved his life. It was

not the first time, as we shall see, that that animating
and arousing word had come, like a relieving army
entering a beleaguered city, to his deliverance. But
the pathos of that heart-breaking yet heart-healing
experience impressed itself indelibly upon his memory; the tale was written in tears; it rushed back
upon him as he lay a-dying; and very often, in the
years that lay between his son's death and his own,
he feelingly referred to it. In July, 1644, for example, I find him writing a letter of sympathy to
Colonel Valentine Walton, whose son has also fallen
on the field of battle. And in this noble yet tender
epistle, Cromwell endeavours to lead the stricken
father to the fountains of consolation at which he
has slaked his own burning thirst. 'Sir,' he says,
'God hath taken away your eldest son by a cannon-
shot. You know my own trials this way, but the
Lord supported me. I remembered that my boy
had entered into the happiness we all pant for and
live for. There, too, is your precious child, full of
glory, never to know sin or sorrow any more. He
was a gallant young man, exceedingly gracious.
God give you His comfort! *You may do all things
through Christ that strengtheneth us.* Seek that,
and you shall easily bear your trial. The Lord be
your strength!'

*'I can do all things through Christ that strength-
eneth me!'*

'This scripture,' he says, as he lies upon his deathbed, *'did once save my life!'*

'Seek that!' he says to Colonel Walton, *'seek that!* seek that!'*

V

But we must go back further yet. We are tracing the stream, but we have not reached the fountainhead. That deathbed testimony at Hampton Court was delivered in 1658. It was in 1639, or thereabouts, that Robert, his eldest son, was lying dead. On each of these occasions the text wonderfully supported him. But, in each case, it came to him as an old friend and not as a new acquaintance. For it was in 1638—the year before Robert's death and twenty years before the father's—that Cromwell wrote to his cousin, Mrs. St. John, about the 'one beam in a dark place that hath such exceedingly great refreshment in it.' When, then, did that beam break upon his darksome path for the first time?

Carlyle thinks that it was in 1623. Cromwell was then in his twenty-fourth year, with all his life before him. But we may as well let Carlyle speak for himself. 'At about this time took place,' he says, 'what Cromwell, with unspeakable joy, would name his conversion. Certainly a grand epoch for a man; properly the one epoch; the turning-point which guides upwards, or guides downwards, him and his activities for evermore! Wilt thou join with the Dragons; wilt thou join with the Gods? Oliver was henceforth a Christian man; believed in

God, not on Sundays only, but on all days, in all places, and in all cases.'

In 1623 it was, then: but how? Piecing the scraps together, a mere hint here and a vague suggestion there, I gather that it was somewhat in this way. In 1623 all things were rushing pellmell towards turgid crisis, wild tumult and red revolution. At home and abroad the outlook was as black as black could be. The world wanted a man, a good man, a great man, a strong man, to save it. Everybody saw the need; but nobody could see the man. Down in Huntingdonshire a young farmer leans on the handles of his plough

'The world needs a man, a good man, a great man, a strong man!' says his Reason. And then he hears another voice.

'Thou art the man!' cries his Conscience, with terrifying suddenness; and his hands tremble as they grasp the plough.

That evening, as he sits beside the fire, his young wife opposite him, and little Robert in the cot by his side, he takes down his Bible and reads. He turns to the epistle to the Philippians, at the closing chapter. He is amazed at the things that, by the grace divine, Paul claims to have learned and achieved.

'It's true, Paul,' he exclaims, 'that *you* have learned this and attained to this measure of grace; but what shall *I* do? Ah, poor creature, it is a hard, hard lesson for me to take out! I find it so!'

Poring over the sacred volume, however, he makes the discovery of his lifetime. 'I came,' he says, 'to the thirteenth verse, where Paul saith, *"I can do all things through Christ which strengtheneth me."* Then faith began to work, and my heart to find comfort and support; and I said to myself, "He that was *Paul's* Christ is *my* Christ too!" And so I drew water out of the Wells of Salvation!'

And now we have reached the fountain-head at last!

VI

And so the clodhopper became the king! It was *the text* that did it! Considered apart from the text, the life of Cromwell is an insoluble mystery, a baffling enigma. But take one good look at the text: observe the place that it occupied in Cromwell's heart and thought: and everything becomes plain. 'That such a man, with the eye to see and with the heart to dare, should advance, from post to post, from victory to victory, till the Huntingdon Farmer became, by whatever name you call him, the acknowledged Strongest Man in England, virtually the King of England, requires,' says Carlyle, 'no magic to explain it.' Of course not! The text explains it. For see!

What is a king? In his *French Revolution,* Carlyle says that the very word 'king' comes from Kon-ning, Can-ning, the Man Who Can, the Man

Who is Able! And that is precisely the burden of the text.

'I can do all things through Christ which strengtheneth me'; so the Authorised Version has it.

'In Him who strengthens me I am able for anything'; so Dr. Moffatt translates the words.

'For all things I am strong in Him who makes me able'; thus Bishop Moule renders it.

A King, says Carlyle, is an Able Man, a Strong Man, a Man who Can. Here is a ploughman who sees that the world is perishing for want of just such a King. How can he, weak as he is, become the world's Strong Man, the world's Able Man, the world's King? The text tells him.

'I can do all things,' he cries, *'through Him that strengtheneth me!'*

The Strong Man was made and the world was saved.

VII

A man—at any rate such a man as Cromwell—can never be content to enjoy such an experience as this alone. No man can read the Life or Letters of the Protector without being touched by his solicitude for others. He is forever anxious that his kindred and friends should drink of those wondrous waters that have so abundantly refreshed and invigorated him. After quoting his text to Colonel Walton, he urges him to seek that same strengthening grace which he himself has received.

'*Seek that!*' he says; '*seek that!*'

It is the keynote of all his correspondence. 'I hope,' he writes to the Mayor of Hursley in 1650, 'I hope you give my son good counsel; I believe he needs it. He is in the dangerous time of his age, and it is a very vain world. O how good it is to close with Christ betimes! There is nothing else worth looking after!'

'*Seek that strength!*' he says to Colonel Walton.

'*Seek that Saviour!*' he says to his wayward son.

'*Seek that which will really satisfy!*' he says to his daughter.

It always seems to me that the old Puritan's lovely letter to that daughter of his, the letter from which I have just quoted, is the gem of Carlyle's great volume. Bridget was twenty-two at the time. 'Your sister,' her father tells her, 'is exercised with some perplexed thoughts. She sees her own vanity and carnal mind, and bewailing it, she seeks after what will satisfy. And thus to be a seeker is to be of the best sect next to a finder, and such an one shall every faithful humble seeker be at the end. Happy seeker; happy finder! Dear heart, press on! Let not husband, let not anything cool thy affections after Christ!'

With which strong, tender, fatherly words from the old soldier to his young daughter we may very well take our leave of him.

IX

FRANCIS XAVIER'S TEXT

It is one of the most stirring dramas of the faith
—a drama in three acts.

I

Scene: 'Neath the Shadow of the Pyrenees.

He is a gay young cavalier. It is the golden age
of Spanish story. Ferdinand and Isabella have
brought the whole world to their feet. Castile
speaks; the peoples tremble; no dog dares bark.
Spain is mistress of mart and of main. Columbus
has just added a new hemisphere to her wide do-
minions. The atmosphere of Europe is trilling
with music and tingling with sensation. And, in
the very year in which the discoverer of America
died, our cavalier is born. His home—a splendid
palace—adorns the pine-clad slopes of the stately
Pyrenees. Its turrets seem to point proudly to the
snow-clad heights that glitter gloriously above. He
was cradled in the lap of luxury. He caught the
spirit of the romantic period, and flung himself with
a will into its revelries and chivalries. Life becomes
a frolic to him. He is a champion in every tussle
for the trophies of the field; he is first in every con-

test for the laurels of the schools. In running and in fencing, in singing and in dancing, he is without a rival. The chalice of life sparkles as he lifts it to his lips, and his eyes gleam as he quaffs the intoxicating cup. In camp, in castle and in court none are more admired, more applauded, more beloved. He is the darling of society. And so, amid scenes of splendour and of gaiety, denied nothing that can minister to his vanity or increase his delight, five-and-thirty years whirl themselves merrily away.

II

Scene: By the Banks of the Seine.

He is in Paris. Even now, in the early part of the sixteenth century, it is a centre of gaiety. He is in his thirty-sixth year. His enthusiasm for pleasure has yielded somewhat to his thirst for knowledge, and his love of learning has begotten a laudable desire to teach. He is lecturing; and among his hearers a strange, ungainly figure hovers in the background. This student of his is a man of fifty, but looks older still. His name is Ignatius Loyola. He is bent and broken, and is pitifully lame. But the fire of a holy enthusiasm burns in his eye. He has marked the brilliant young teacher for his own, and is determined to win him. He makes friends. After each utterance he congratulates the lecturer, and adds significantly: *'But what shall it profit a man if he gain the whole world and lose his own soul?'*

The whole world! His own soul!

To gain the world! To lose his soul!

'What shall it profit a man if he gain the whole world and lose his own soul?'

He lounges with the lecturer in the solitude of the study, he accompanies him in his evening walks along the banks of the Seine; they explore together the dense woodlands which occupy the site of future Parisian suburbs. But whether in springtide rambles among the lilies and the daffodils, or in riverside strolls by sunset, or in halls of feasting and music and pleasure, or in silent study, or in the stately academy, the strange student asks, and repeats, and asks again one incessant question:

'But what shall it profit a man if he gain the whole world and lose his own soul?'

The whole world! His own soul!

To gain the world! To lose his soul!

'But what shall it profit a man if he gain the whole world and lose his own soul?'

A hundred times, as he painfully hobbles along beside his brilliant young master, the deformed pupil reiterates his unanswerable query. And at last, the master mind capitulates to the pitiless and resistless logic of that immortal question. The great professor becomes the lowliest of penitents. Student and lecturer kneel side by side, and, in a tempest of tears, the young lecturer dedicates all that is left of life to that Saviour into whose awful presence his student has ushered him. The lecturer has learned more from his listener than he could ever have imparted.

III

Scene· On the Seashore of Siam.

He is a monk. His face is drawn with suffering. Fasts and vigils have left their mark. But. great as are the tortures of his body, the anguish of his mind is greater still. Having himself heard the Story of the Cross, a new idea haunts and possesses him. He is horrified by the fearful reflection that the nations sit in darkness and know not the light which has irradiated him. Not a moment must be lost! Thousands are dropping daily into Christless graves! It is an alarming and terrifying discovery! He will set out at once, and the peoples shall hear from his own lips the story of redeeming love! There are no trains or coaches. He will tramp through the world till his limbs are swollen and his nerves are numb. He sets out. He visits India, and hastening from province to province, picks up the languages as he goes along by happy intercourse with little children. He stands one day amidst the dazzling splendour of an Oriental palace; on the next, he pays court to a rajah and his native staff; on the third he moves amongst the filthy huts of the fisher-folk of Malabar. But every day, and everywhere, he tells with agony and tears, his strange and wondrous tale. Ridiculed, stoned and persecuted, he presses tirelessly on, always uplifting the Cross with his right hand, and with his left, ringing the bell that summons the people to attend. Having made converts, and planted churches, he loses not an hour, but hurries off in search of fresh fields to add to his Divine conquest. He labours for twenty-one hours out of every twenty-four. In the course of ten short years he learns and preaches in twenty different languages. Now he begs a passage in a troopship, and anon he sails with idolatrous pirates and blasphemous corsairs. He tumbles about the oceans in vessels that would not now be permitted to navigate a river. And at sea, as on land, the passion of his sacred purpose consumes him still. He haunts the forecastle, pleading, one by one, with every soldier and sailor on the troopship. He proclaims to robbers and to slaves the glowing words of life eternal. Across burning deserts and over snowy ranges he threads his fearless way. The fierce blaze of equatorial suns, and the piercing cold of slippery mountain glaciers, alike fail to baffle or deter him. He throws himself into scenes of battle and of carnage that he may strive for the souls of the wounded and the dying. Whilst the very earth rocks beneath his feet, he stands on the shuddering slopes of blazing volcanoes that, amidst scenes of exquisite and majestic horror, he may urge the panic-stricken natives to flee from the wrath to come. He visits

leper settlements, and, with all the tenderness of a
woman, nurses hideous human wrecks the very sight
of whom would sicken a less intrepid spirit. He
boards ships whose crews are perishing of loathsome
pestilence, and, unafraid of contracting their disgust-
ing maladies, he ministers to the diseased, and kneels
beside the prostrate forms of the dying. He comes
like a ghost upon wild, untutored inland tribes; he
bursts into the island territories of fierce and un-
tamed cannibals. He invades the secret lair of the
bandit, and penetrates to the lonely tent of the Bed-
ouin. He passes spectrally from shore to shore.
He startles armies on the march, and arrests the
progress of the journeying caravan. His limbs are
often paralysed with fatigue. He tramps across
continents until, from sheer exhaustion, he drops
upon the hard and inhospitable soil; and then,
having rested for an hour, he rises and staggers on
again. He dares death in every form; he shakes
hands with every ailment and disease; he endures all
the pangs of hunger and all the horrors of thirst;
he suffers desolating shipwreck and bitter persecution. He can rejoice in any privation if he may but
uplift the Cross on every shore, and preach the
gospel to every creature. And it is always observed
that, on whatever coast he lands, and in whatever
language he preaches, whether he addresses the
nabobs of Mysore or the Mikado of Japan, whether
he speaks on the deck of a pirate or in the hovel of
a slave, he echoes endlessly one everlasting question:

'*But what shall it profit a man if he gain the whole world and lose his own soul?*'

The whole world! His own soul!

To gain the world! To lose his soul!

'*What shall it profit a man if he gain the whole world and lose his own soul?*'

At last, absolutely worn out after ten short strenuous years, at the age of forty-five, he lays his wasted, worn, emaciated frame upon the sea-beach of Siam, and, unnursed and untended, resigns his soul to God. He dies, as he lived, with a smile upon his face. His winsomeness was as wonderful as his daring. Little children simply revelled in his company. His life is the most stinging rebuke that history has ever administered to apathy. His record is a stimulus to every church, and a challenge to every age. It must quicken the blood, and fire the fervour, of good men till his great Master come. It will accelerate the triumphant progress of all noble enterprises till time shall be no more.

*   *   *   *   *   *

And the rest of the acts of Francis Xavier, and all that he did, and the things that he suffered, and the peoples that he reached, and the churches that he planted, are they not written in the book of the Chronicles of Christendom?

X

J. B. GOUGH'S TEXT

I

HE is an old man of twenty-five! Nobody, seeing him to-night, would suspect that he had seen so few winters; and nobody would suspect that forty-four summers, filled with sunshine and with song, lie between him and his grave. Here he sits at a bare table, in an empty, cheerless room. He shivers, for he is hungry, and he is insufficiently clad. His thin arms are folded on the table, and his haggard face rests upon them. He feels that he has come to the fag-end of everything. He has just completed seven dark and dreadful years. 'During those years,' as he himself tells us, with a shudder, in the brighter after-days, 'during those years I wandered over God's beautiful earth like an unblessed spirit. It was like being driven by whips across a burning desert: I was for ever digging deep wells to quench my maddening thirst, and for ever bringing up nothing but the hot, dry sand! Seven years of darkness! Seven years of slavery! Seven years of dissipation! Seven years of sin!'

But let us not be too swift to pity! Pity, like charity, must be intelligent; it is too sacred a thing to be wasted or squandered. It does not follow, because this man is ragged and wretched, that he is therefore poor. He is rich; and it is only in such extremities of distress that men discover their buried wealth. To-night, sitting in despair within this squalid room, he suddenly finds himself possessed of incalculable treasure! Memory yields up her golden hoard! There rush back upon him the tender, hallowed, clustering associations of his early days: the village church, the Sunday School, and, best of all, the dear old English home. As he sits here in this squalid room, his outer-self is on one side of the Atlantic whilst his inmost soul is on the other. His gaunt frame, disfigured by the life that he has lived, is in Massachusetts; but his heart, flying on the wings of fancy, is back among the sweet and fragrant fields of his Kentish home. And, the centre and soul of all those radiant recollections, he sees the sad and wistful face of his mother. His face is still buried in his ragged sleeves, so the tears do not show; but they are there.

'Oh, that mother of mine!' Gough used to say; 'she was one of Christ's nobility, and she possessed a patent signed and sealed with His redeeming blood! She was poor in purse, but rich in piety; a brave, godly woman! She died a pauper and was buried without a shroud and without a prayer; but she left her children a legacy that has made them wealthier than peers and princes! I remember one night, towards the close of her life, sitting with her in the garret, and we had no candle.

She said to me, "John, I am growing blind; I don't feel it much; but you are young, and it is hard for you to have a poor, blind mother. But never mind, John; there is no night in heaven and no need of any candle there; the Lamb is the light thereof!" Oh, that mother of mine! She is neither poor nor blind now; she has left that dark and gloomy garret to bask in the sunshine of her Saviour's smiles!' And it was his mother, or at least the fond, clear memory of his mother, that came to his relief in the hour of his most dire extremity. That is a way that mothers have! But let him tell the story in his own way.

'All at once,' he says, 'it seemed as if the very light she left as she passed had spanned the dark chasm of those seven dreadful years, struck the heart, and opened it. The passages of Scripture that she had taught me, and that had been buried in my memory, came to me as if they were being whispered in my ear by the loving lips of my mother herself. *"He is able to save to the uttermost them that come unto God by Him."* It is the very thing I need! I want to be saved—I cannot save myself—*He is able to save to the uttermost!*—Then He is the Saviour for me!'

I said that, poor as he seemed, this youth of twenty-five owned *'buried* treasure'!

That text, he says, was *'buried* in my memory!'

'He is able to save to the uttermost them that come unto God by Him!'

See, he rises at last; draws his sleeve across his eyes; pulls himself together; and, clutching at that text as a drowning man clutches at his rescuer's hand, he walks out of that cheerless room in the power of an endless life.

II

This, then, was J. B. Gough's text. Not that he held any proprietary rights in it. John Bunyan would dispute any such pretensions. 'At another time,' says Bunyan, 'I was much under this question. *Whether the blood of Christ was sufficient to save my soul?* in which doubt I continued from morning till about seven or eight at night: and at last, when I was, as it were, quite worn out with fear, lest it should not lay hold on me, these words did sound suddenly within my heart: *"He is able."* But methought, this word *"able"* was spoke loud unto me; it showed *a great word,* it seemed to be writ in *great letters,* and gave such a jostle to my fear and doubt as I never had before or after. For *"He is able to save to the uttermost them that come unto God by Him."* '

'Is there salvation for me, even for me?' asks J. B. Gough, in his despair.

'Is the blood of Christ sufficient to save my soul, even mine?' asks John Bunyan, in that anxious hour.

And to both of them there came the same reply: *'He is able to save to the uttermost!'*

'It is a great word!' says Gough.

'It seems to be writ in great letters!' says Bunyan.

And by that gallant and assuring word they were both greatly delivered.

III

In the fairy story that beguiled our infancy, the Three Giants confronted the hero just as he was setting out on his romantic quest. J. B. Gough had a precisely similar experience. On the very threshold of the new life three tyrannical figures arose and endeavoured to drive him back to slavery. Their names? The name of the first was *Yesterday;* the name of the second was *To-day;* and the name of the third was *To-morrow.*

Giant Yesterday pointed out with terrific emphasis that the past is absolutely indelible. What's done can never be undone! There are some things that even God cannot do; and this is one of them.

> Wounds of the soul, though healed, will ache;
> The reddening scars remain
>   And make confession;
> Lost innocence returns no more;
> We are not what we were
>   Before transgression!

To the end of his days, Gough was haunted by the grim ghosts of those seven terrible and remorseless years. 'I have suffered,' he cried, 'and come out of the fire scorched and scathed with the marks upon my person and with the memory of it

burnt right into my soul!' He likened his life to a
snowdrift that had been sadly stained. No power
on earth can restore its former purity and whiteness. 'The scars remain! the scars remain!' he
used to say, with bitter self-reproaches. Giant
Yesterday pointed to the black, black past derisively;
held it as a threat over the poor penitent's bowed
and contrite head; and told him in tones that sounded
like thunder-claps that there was no escape.

Giant To-day points to things as they are: 'Look
at yourself!' the tyrant exclaims. 'Facts are facts;
your present condition is a fact; how can you evade
it?' Gough throws himself back in a chair and gives
rein to his fancy. A vision, or, rather, a series of
visions, come to him. Before him stands a bright,
fair-haired, blue-eyed, beautiful boy, with rosy
cheeks and pearly teeth and ruby lip—the perfect
picture of innocence and peace, health, purity and
joy.

'Who are you?' Gough asked.

'I am your Past; I am what you *Were!*'

Another figure appears. The youth has become
a man. He looks born to command. Intellect
flashes from the eye; the noble brow speaks of
genius trained and consecrated; it is a glorious
spectacle.

'And who are you!' Gough asks again.

'I am your Ideal; I am what you *Might Have
Been!*' Then there creeps slowly into the bare room
a wretched thing, unkempt and loathsome, it is

manacled, hard and fast; the face is furrowed and
filthy; the lip is swollen and repulsive; the brow is
branded as the throne of sensuality; the eyes glare
wildly and are bleared and dim.

'And who are you?' Gough again demands.

'I am your Present; I am what you *Are!*' By
this expressive shadow-show, Giant To-day sought
to frighten a trembling spirit from its rich inherit-
ance.

And as for Giant To-morrow, his case is ready-
made. 'It is easy enough to be religious to-day,'
he says, 'but what of to-morrow, and the next day,
and all the days that are coming? If one temptation fails to overthrow you, another will surely
bring you down!' And Gough, who knows the cruel
strength of each temptation, feels the force of what
these monsters say.

IV

The Three Giants withdraw, leaving Gough in
the depths of despair. How can he venture upon
the Christian life? He has only to review his own
indelible Past; he has only to contemplate his hu-
miliating Present; he has only to conjure up the
sinister probabilities of the unpromising Future, in
order to recognise the sheer audacity of such a step.
Can he reasonably hope to keep his vow through all
the years ahead? Many a race is lost at the last lap;
many a ship is wrecked on the reefs outside its final
port; many a battle is lost on the last charge; what

hope has he of completing the course upon which he proposes to venture? He feels that it is hopelessly beyond him.

And it is at this critical juncture that the text comes bravely to his rescue.

'I am not able!' moans the distracted penitent.

'*He* is able!' replies the text.

'I should falter before I had finished!' says Gough.

'He is able to save *to the uttermost*,' answers the text. To the uttermost—to the very last inch of the very last yard of the very last mile! To the uttermost—to the very last minute of the very last hour of the very last day! '*He is able to save to the uttermost them that come unto God by Him, seeing He ever liveth to make intercession for them.*'

And thus the Three Giants are discomfited and put to confusion. And Gough enters into a peace that only becomes deeper and fuller and richer and sweeter as the long and busy years go by.

V   .

Every man carries in his soul a note of exclamation and a note of interrogation. But we do not place them similarly. The leper in the Gospels put the note of exclamation against the *ability* of Christ to cleanse him, and the note of interrogation against His *willingness* to save. 'If Thou wilt, Thou canst make me whole!'

Thou canst!!!
If Thou wilt???

Most of us find the prevailing wind blowing from the opposite quarter. We give the Saviour credit for a certain amiable *willingness* to help us; but, knowing as we do all that the Three Giants have to say, we doubt His *ability* to deliver. We put the notes of exclamation and of interrogation the other way.

Thou wilt!!!
If Thou canst???

But, as J. B. Gough discovered on that never-to-be-forgetten day, the Christian message is a revelation of a limitless ability to deliver. It is never a try; it is always a triumph. We have witnessed this desperate struggle in a squalid room at Massachusetts—the struggle of an enslaved soul after freedom. Let us go back a hundred years. Exactly a century before this scene was enacted in an American attic, a dramatic episode marked the historic ministry of Philip Doddridge at Northampton. An Irishman named Connell was convicted of a capital offence and sentenced to be publicly hanged. Mr. Doddridge, at great trouble and expense, instituted a most rigid scrutiny, and proved, beyond the possibility of a doubt, that Connell was a hundred and twenty miles away when the crime was committed. The course of judgement could not, however, be deflected. Connell was asked if he had any request to make before setting out for the gallows. He answered that he desired the procession to pause in front of the house of Mr. Philip Doddridge, that he might kneel on the minister's doorstep and pray for the man who had tried to save him.

'Mr. Doddridge,' he cried, when the procession halted, 'every hair of my head thanks you; every throb of my heart thanks you; every drop of my blood thanks you; for you did your best to save me!'

Mr. Doddridge *was willing to save.*

Mr. Doddridge *did his best to save.*

Mr. Doddridge was *not able to save.*

But *'He is able to save to the uttermost them that come unto God by Him!'* That is the glory of the Gospel that won the heart of Gough that day and held him a glad captive through all the fruitful years that followed.

VI

Mr. Chesterton says that 'God paints in many colours, but He never paints so gorgeously as when He paints in white.' The crimson of the sunset; the azure of the ocean; the green of the valleys; the scarlet of the poppies; the silver of the dewdrops; the gold of the gorse; these are exquisite—so perfectly beautiful, indeed, that we cannot imagine an attractive heaven without them. God paints in many colours; but in the soul of J. B. Gough He paints in white; and we feel that here the divine art is at its very best. Forty-four crowded and productive years have passed since that grim struggle in the squalid room. Gough is again in America, addressing a vast audience of young men at Philadelphia.

'Young men,' he cries, perhaps with a bitter memory of those seven indelible years, 'Young men, keep your record clean!'

He pauses: it is a longer pause than usual; and the audience wonders. But he regains his voice.

'Young men,' he repeats more feebly this time, 'keep your record clean!'

Another pause, longer than before. But again he finds the power of speech.

'Young men,' he cries a third time, but in a thin, wavering voice, 'young men, keep your record clean!'

He falls heavily on the platform. Devout men carry him to his burial, and make lamentation over him. His race is finished; his voyage completed; his battle won. The promise has been literally and triumphantly fulfilled. The grace that saved him has kept him to the very last inch of the very last yard of the very last mile; to the very last minute of the very last hour of the very last day; for 'He is able to save *to the uttermost* them that come unto God by Him!'

XI

JOHN KNOX'S TEXT

I

SOME men are not born to die. It is their prerogative to live; they come on purpose. A thousand deaths will not lay them in a grave. No disease from within, no danger from without, can by any means destroy them. They bear upon their faces the stamp of the immortal. In more senses than one, they come into the world for good. Among such deathless men John Knox stands out conspicuously. When in Edinburgh it is impossible to believe that John Knox lived four hundred years ago. He is so very much alive to-day that it seems incredible that he was living even then. The people will show you his grave in the middle of the road, and the meagre epitaph on the flat tombstone will do its feeble best to convince you that his voice has been silent for centuries; but you will sceptically shake your head and move away. For, as you walk about the noble and romantic city, John Knox is everywhere! He is the most ubiquitous man you meet. You come upon him at every street corner. Here is the house in which he dwelt; there is the church in which he preached; at every turn you come upon places that are haunted by him still. The very stones vibrate with the strident accents of his voice; the walls echo to his footsteps. I was introduced to quite a number of people in Edinburgh; but I blush to confess that I have forgotten them all—*all but John Knox.* It really seems to me, looking back upon that visit, that I met John Knox somewhere or other every five minutes. I could hear the ring of his voice; I could see the flash of his eye; I could feel the impress of his huge and commanding personality. The tomb in the middle of the road notwithstanding, John Knox is indisputably the most virile force in Scotland at this hour. I dare say that, like me, he sometimes catches sight of that tomb in the middle of the road. If so, he laughs—as he could laugh—and strides defiantly on. For John Knox was born in 1505 and, behold, he liveth and abideth for ever!

II

John Knox, I say, was born in 1505. In 1505, therefore, Scotland was born again. For the birth of such a man is the regeneration of a nation. Life in Knox was not only immortal; it was contagious. Because of Knox, Carlyle affirms, the people began to live! 'In the history of Scotland,' says Carlyle, himself a Scotsman, 'in the history of Scotland I can find but one epoch: it contains nothing of world-interest at all, but this Reformation by Knox.' But surely, surely, the sage is nodding! Has Carlyle forgotten Sir Walter Scott and Robert Burns and all Scotland's noble contribution to literature, to in-

dustry, to religion and to life? But Carlyle will not
retract or modify a single word. 'This that Knox
did for his nation,' he goes on, 'was a resurrection
as from death. The people began to live! Scotch
literature and thought, Scotch industry; James Watt,
David Hume, Walter Scott, Robert Burns: I find
John Knox acting in the heart's core of every one
of these persons and phenomena; I find that without
him they would not have been.' So much have I
said in order to show that, beyond the shadow of
a doubt, if a text made John Knox, then that text
made history.

III

'Go!' said the old reformer to his wife, as he
lay a-dying, and the words were his last, 'go, read
where I cast my first anchor!' She needed no more
explicit instructions, for he had told her the story
again and again. It is Richard Bannatyne, Knox's
serving-man, who has placed the scene on record.
'On November 24, 1572,' he says, 'John Knox departed this life to his eternal rest. Early in the
afternoon he said, "Now, for the last time, I com-
mend my spirit, soul and body"—pointing upon his
three fingers—"into Thy hands, O Lord!" There-
after, about five o'clock, he said to his wife, "Go,
read where I cast my first anchor!" She did not
need to be told, and so she read the seventeenth of
John's evangel.' Let us listen as she reads it! '*Thou
hast given Him authority over all flesh, that He*

should give eternal life to as many as Thou hast given Him, and this is life eternal, that they might know Thee, the only true God, and Jesus Christ whom Thou hast sent.'

Here was a strange and striking contrast!

'Eternal Life! Life Eternal!' says the Book.

Now listen to the laboured breathing from the bed!

The Bed speaks of Death; the Book speaks of Life Everlasting!

'Life!' the dying man starts as the great cadences fall upon his ear.

'This is Life Eternal, that they might *know Thee!'*

'Life Eternal!'

'It was *there*,' he declares with his last breath, 'it was *there* that I cast my first anchor!'

IV

How was that first anchor cast? I have tried to piece the records together. Paul never forgot the day on which he saw Stephen stoned; John Knox never forgot the day on which he saw George Wishart burned. Wishart was a man 'of such grace'— so Knox himself tells us—'as before him was never heard within this realm.' He was regarded with an awe that was next door to superstition, and with an affection that was almost adoration. Are we not told that in the days when the plague lay over Scotland, 'the people of Dundee saw it approaching from the west in the form of a great black cloud?

They fell on their knees and prayed, crying to the cloud to pass them by, but even while they prayed it came nearer. Then they looked around for the most holy man among them, to intervene with God on their behalf. All eyes turned to George Wishart, and he stood up, stretching his arms to the cloud, and prayed, and it rolled back.' Out on the borders of the town, however, the pestilence was raging, and Wishart, hastening thither, took up his station on the town wall, preaching to the plague-stricken on the one side of him and to the healthy on the other, and exhibiting such courage and intrepidity in grappling with the awful scourge that he became the idol of the grateful people. In 1546, however, he was convicted of heresy and burned at the foot of the Castle Wynd, opposite the Castle Gate. When he came near to the fire, Knox tells us, he sat down upon his knees, and repeated aloud some of the most touching petitions from the Psalms. As a sign of forgiveness, he kissed the executioner on the cheek, saying: 'Lo, here is a token that I forgive thee. My harte, do thine office!' The faggots were kindled, and the leaping flames bore the soul of Wishart triumphantly skywards.

V

And there, a few yards off, stands Knox! Have a good look at him! He is a man 'rather under middle height, with broad shoulders, swarthy face, black hair, and a beard of the same colour a span and a half long. He has heavy eyebrows, eyes deeply sunk, cheekbones prominent and cheeks ruddy. The mouth is large, the lips full, especially the upper one. The whole aspect of the man is not unpleasing; and, in moments of emotion, it is invested with an air of dignity and majesty.' Knox could never shake from his sensitive mind the tragic yet triumphant scene near the Castle Gate; and when, many years afterwards, he himself turned aside to die, he repeated with closed eyes the prayers that he had heard George Wishart offer under the shadow of the stake.

Was it *then*, I wonder, that John Knox turned sadly homeward and read to himself the great High Priestly prayer in 'the seventeenth of John's evangel'? Was it on that memorable night that he caught a glimpse of the place which all the redeemed hold in the heart of the Redeemer? Was it on that melancholy evening that there broke upon him the revelation of a love that enfolded not only his martyred friend and himself, but the faithful of every time and of every clime? Was it *then* that he opened his heart to the magic and the music of those tremendous words: '*Thou hast given Him authority over all flesh, that He should give eternal life to as many as Thou hast given Him; and this is life eternal, that they might know Thee, the only true God, and Jesus Christ whom Thou hast sent.*' Was it *then?* I cannot say for certain. I only know that we never meet with Knox in Scottish story until

after the maryrdom of Wishart; and I know that,
by the events of that sad and tragic day, all his soul
was stirred within him.   But, although I do not
know for certain that the anchor was first cast *then,*
I know that it was first cast *there.* 'Go!' he said,
with the huskiness of death upon his speech, 'read
me where I cast my first anchor!' And his wife
straightway read to him the stately sentences I have
just re-written.

'*Life Eternal!*'

'*This is Life Eternal!*'

'*This* is Life Eternal, that they might *know Thee!*'

'It was there, *there,* THERE, that I cast my first
anchor!'

VI

Fierce as were the storms that beat upon Knox
during the great historic years that followed, that
anchor bravely held.   To say nothing of his experiences at Court and the powerful efforts to coax
or to cow him into submission, think of those twelve
years of exile, eighteen months of which were spent
on the French galleys.   We catch two furtive
glimpses of him.   The galley in which he is chained
makes a cruise round the Scottish coast.   It passes
so near to the fair fields of Fife that Knox can dis-
tinctly see the spires of St. Andrew's.   At the
moment, Knox was so ill that his life was despaired
of; and the taunting vision might well have broken
his spirit altogether.   But the anchor held; the an-

chor held! 'Ah!' exclaimed Knox, raising himself
on his elbow, 'I see the steeple of that place where
God first in public opened my mouth to His glory;
and I am fully persuaded, how weak soever I now
appear, that I shall not depart this life till that my
tongue shall glorify His godly name in the same
place' Again, as Carlyle tells, 'a priest one day
presented to the galley-slaves an image of the Virgin
Mother, requiring that they, the blasphemous here-
tics, should do it reverence. "Mother? Mother of
God?" said Knox, when the turn came to him, "This
is no Mother of God; this is a piece of painted wood!
She is better for swimming, I think, than for being
worshipped!" and he flung the thing into the river.'
Knox had cast his anchor in the seventeenth of
John's evangel.

'This is life eternal, that they might know
Thee!'

And since he had himself found life eternal in the
personal friendship of a Personal Redeemer, it was
intolerable to him that others should gaze with su-
perstitious eyes on 'a bit of painted wood.'

The thing fell into the river with a splash. It
was a rude jest, but an expressive one. All the
Reformation was summed up in it. Eternal life
was not to be found in such things. '*This* is life
eternal, that they might know *Thee.*' That, says
Knox, is where I cast my first anchor; and, through
all the storm and stress of those baffling and eventful
years, that anchor held!

VII

Nor was there any parting of the cable or dragging of the anchor at the last. Richard Bannatyne, sitting beside his honoured master's deathbed, heard a long, long sigh. A singular fancy overtook him.

'Now, sir,' he said, 'the time to end your battle has come. Remember those comfortable promises of our Saviour Jesus Christ which you have so often shown to us. And it may be that, when your eyes are blind and your ears deaf to every other sight and sound, you will still be able to recognise my voice. I shall bend over you and ask if you have still the hope of glory. Will you promise that, if you are able to give me some signal, you will do so?'

The sick man promised, and, soon after, this is what happened:

Grim in his deep death-anguish the stern old champion lay,
And the locks upon his pillow were floating thin and grey,
And, visionless and voiceless, with quick and labouring breath,
He waited for his exit through life's dark portal, Death.

'Hast thou the hope of glory?' They bowed to catch the
    thrill
That through some languid token might be responsive still,
Nor watched they long nor waited for some obscure reply,
He raised a clay-cold finger, and pointed to the sky.

So the death-angel found him, what time his bow he bent,
To give the struggling spirit a sweet enfranchisement.
So the death-angel left him, what time earth's bonds were
    riven,
The cold, stark, stiffening finger still pointing up to heaven.

'He had a sore fight of an existence,' says Carlyle,
'wrestling with Popes and Principalities; in defeat,
contention, life-long struggle; rowing as a galley-
slave, wandering as an exile. A sore fight: but he
won it! "Have you hope?" they asked him in his
last moment, when he could no longer speak. He
lifted his finger, pointed upward, and so died!
Honour to him! His works have not died. The
letter of his work dies, as of all men's; but the spirit
of it, never.' Did I not say in my opening sentences
that John Knox was among the immortal humans?
When he entered the world, he came into it for good!

VIII

'*This* is life eternal, that they might *know Thee!*'
'That,' says Knox, with his dying breath, 'that is
where I cast my first anchor!' It is a sure anchor-
age, O heart of mine! Cast thine anchor there!
Cast thine anchor in the oaths and covenants of the
Most High! Cast thine anchor in His infallible, im-
mutable, unbreakable Word! Cast thine anchor in
the infinite love of God! Cast thine anchor in the
redeeming grace of Christ! Cast thine anchor in
the everlasting Gospel! Cast thine anchor in the
individual concern of the individual Saviour for the
individual soul! Cast thine anchor there; and, come
what may, that anchor will always hold!

XII

WILLIAM COWPER'S TEXT

I

HAVE a good look at him, this shy, shuddering, frail little fellow of six, for rough hands are waiting to hustle him on to the coach and to pack him off to a distant boarding-school! He is a quivering little bundle of nerves; slight of figure; with pale, pinched face, and eyes swollen with chronic inflammation. He starts at every sound in the daytime, and throws the bedclothes over his head at night that he may not be scared to death by the ghostly shadows that flit across the wall. His mother, his sole source of comfort, has just died: that is why he is being sent away from home. The memory of her was ever afterwards the one star that illumined his dark sky. Late in his life, a picture of her was presented to him; and his ecstasy knew no bounds. 'The world,' he wrote to the giver, 'could not have furnished you with a present so acceptable to me as the picture which you have so kindly sent me I received it the night before last, and received it with a trepidation of nerves and spirits somewhat akin to what I should have felt had its dear original presented herself to my embrace. I kissed it and hung it where it is the last object which I see at night, and the first on which I open my eyes in the morning. Her memory is to me dear beyond expression.' And then, turning to the picture itself, he breaks into poetry:

Oh, that those lips had language! Life has passed
With me but roughly since I heard thee last.
Those lips are thine—thy own sweet smile I see,
The same that oft in childhood solaced me.
My mother, when I learn'd that thou wast dead,
Say, wast thou conscious of the tears I shed?
Perhaps thou gav'st me, though unfelt, a kiss;
Perhaps a tear, if souls can weep in bliss.
I heard the bell toll'd on thy burial day;
I saw the hearse that bore thee slow away
Thy maidens, grieved themselves at my concern,
Oft gave me promise of thy quick return.
Thus many a sad to-morrow came and went,
Till, all my stock of infant sorrow spent,
I learn'd at last submission to my lot,
But, though I less deplored thee, ne'er forgot!

So his mother dies and leaves him—a queer, unwelcome heritage—to his father. And his father, utterly bewildered by the boy's odd fancies and erratic ways, has resolved to get out of the difficulty by banishing him to a boarding-school. At the boarding-school he is badgered and bullied and beaten without respite and without mercy; and to the last day of his life he never thinks of the horrid place without a shudder.

Have a good look at him, I say, before they bundle him into the cavernous interior of the old coach. For, in spite of everything, this little parcel of timid, quivering sensibility is going to make history. It frequently happens that, when a man drops into his grave, his fame gradually subsides until his memory entirely perishes. With Cowper a diametrically opposite principle has been at work. More than a century has elapsed since he quitted the scene of his labours; and during that period the lustre of his fame has steadily grown. Time was when it was the fashion to pooh-pooh the claims of Cowper. 'Did he not,' it was asked contemptuously, 'did he not on several occasions attempt suicide and spend much of his time in a mad-house?' This, of course, is indisputable; but it is also true that almost any young fellow of nervous temperament and frail constitution would lose his reason, and seek some violent means of escape from the horrors of life, if his malady were treated as it was customary to treat such cases a century and a half ago. The marvel is that from so frail a personality, so pitilessly treated, we have inherited poetry that will be cherished as long as the language lasts.

II

It is the glory of Cowper that he stands among our pioneers. England had wrapped herself in gloomy and sullen silence. Literary genius seemed dead. Then, all at once, the country became like a grove at sunrise. And the first note heard was the note of William Cowper. Dr. Arnold, in talking to his boys at Rugby, used to call him 'the singer of the dawn.' Goldwin Smith declares that he is the

most important poet between the time of Pope and
the time of Wordsworth. In one of his best essays,
Macaulay says that Byron contributed more than
any other writer, more even than Sir Walter Scott,
to the literary brilliance of the period; and he is
careful to emphasize the fact that it was Cowper who
called that fruitful era into being. 'Cowper,' he
says, 'was the forerunner of the great restoration
of our literature;' and a little further on he declares
that, 'during the twenty years which followed the
death of Cowper, the revolution in English poetry
was fully consummated.' So there he stands, holding, and holding for all time, a place peculiarly his
own in our British life and letters. He is an attractive, if a somewhat depressing, figure. A feeble,
sensitive and highly-strung physique; a mental
wreck; a would-be suicide; a passionate lover of all
forms of animal life; the author of some of our
quaintest humour and some of our most sacred
hymns; his life was, as Byron expressively said, a
singular pendulum, swinging ever between a smile
and a tear. Few poets are more human, more simple, more unaffected, more restful than he; few are
more easy to read. His 'John Gilpin,' his 'Alexander
Selkirk,' his 'Boadicea,' and 'My Mother's Picture'
were among the first poems we learned in our school-
books; some of his verses will be among the last
we shall care to remember. Perhaps his most force-
ful and pathetic epitaph was written by Mrs. Brown-
ing, in words as true as they are sorrowful:—

O poets, from a maniac's tongue was poured the deathless
    singing!
O Christians, at your cross of hope a hopeless hand was
    clinging!
O men, this man in brotherhood your weary paths beguiling,
Groaned inly while he taught you peace, and died while you
    were smiling!

III

But it is time that we asked ourselves a question.
What was it that so distracted this sensitive brain?
What was it that almost broke this gentle and cling-
ing spirit? What was it that again and again drove
Cowper to attempt his own destruction? There is
only one answer. It was his sin. 'My sin; my sin!'
he cries from morning till night, and, very often,
from night until morning. 'Oh, for some fountain
open for sin and uncleanness!' But he can find no
such fountain anywhere. He is like the old lama,
in Kipling's *Kim,* who was continually searching for
the River, the River of the Arrow, the River that
can cleanse from sin! But, like the lama, he can
nowhere find those purifying waters. And because
his frenzied quest is so fruitless and so hopeless, he
seeks relief in a premature death. But every rash
attempt fails, and, failing, adds to his consternation;
for he feels that, in attempting suicide, he has committed the unpardonable sin, and his plight is a thousand times worse than it was before. He has been
told of the Fountain, but he can never find it. He
has been told of the Lamb of God that taketh away
the sin of the world; but he knows not how to ap-

proach Him. He longs for 'a light to shine upon the road that leads us to the Lamb,' but the darkness only grows more dense. Then, when the blackness of the night seems impenetrable, day suddenly breaks!

IV

Cowper is a patient at Dr. Cotton's private lunatic asylum. In those days such asylums usually broke the bruised reed and quenched the smoking flax. But, happily for William Cowper and the world, Dr. Cotton's is the exception. Dr. Cotton is himself a kindly, gracious and devout old man; and he treats his poor patient with sympathy and understanding. And, under this treatment, the change comes. Cowper rises one morning feeling better: he grows cheerful over his breakfast; takes up the Bible, which in his fits of madness he always threw aside, and, opening it at random, lights upon a passage that breaks upon him like a burst of glorious sunshine. Let him tell the story. 'The happy period which was to shake off my fetters and afford me a clear opening of the free mercy of God in Christ Jesus was now arrived. I flung myself into a chair near the window, and, seeing a Bible there, ventured once more to apply to it for comfort and instruction. The first verses I saw were in the third of Romans: *"Being justified freely by His grace through the redemption that is in Christ Jesus, whom God hath set forth to be a propitiation, through faith in His blood, to manifest His righteousness."* Immediately I received strength to believe, and the full beams of the Sun of Righteousness shone upon me. I saw the sufficiency of the atonement He had made, my pardon in His blood, and the fulness and completeness of His justification. In a moment I believed and received the gospel.'

Side by side with this illuminating experience of Cowper's let me set a strikingly similar experience which befel John Bunyan exactly a hundred years before. To the soul of Bunyan the self-same text brought the self-same deliverance. 'Now,' he says, 'my soul was clogged with guilt, and was greatly pinched between these two considerations, Live I must not, die I dare not. Now I sunk and fell in my spirit, and was giving up all for lost; but as I was walking up and down in the house, as a man in a most woeful state, that word of God took hold of my heart, *"Ye are justified freely by His grace, through the redemption that is in Christ Jesus, whom God hath set forth to be a propitiation, through faith in His blood, to manifest His righteousness."* Oh, what a turn it made upon me! I was as one awakened out of some troublesome dream.'

V

'*What a turn it made upon me!*' says John Bunyan in 1656.

'*What a turn it made upon me!*' says William Cowper in 1756.

For the argument of that great text is irresistible. If the love of God be so great as to provide such a Saviour, how could He be eager for the condemnation of the guiltiest? If the grace of God be so freely outpoured in justifying energy, how could any man be beyond the pale of hope? And if God is so anxious for the salvation of men that He has set forth—underlined, emphasised, explained, made bravely prominent—this propitiation, why should even the most timorous of mortals draw back in terror?

For Cowper, from that moment, the whole world was changed. 'Huntingdon,' says one of his biographers, 'seemed a paradise. The heart of its new inhabitant was full of the unspeakable happiness that comes with calm after storm, with health after the most terrible of maladies, with repose after the burning fever of the brain. When first he went to Church, he was in a spiritual ecstasy; it was with difficulty that he restrained his emotions; though his voice was silent, being stopped by the intensity of his feelings, his heart within him sang for joy; and when the gospel for the day was read, the sound of it was more than he could bear. This brightness of his mind communicated itself to all the objects around him, to the sluggish waters of the Ouse, to dull, fenny Huntingdon, and to its commonplace inhabitants.'

'What a turn it made upon me!' says Bunyan in 1656.

'What a turn it made upon me!' says Cowper in
1756. And again he breaks into poetry:

> I was a stricken deer that left the herd
> Long since; with many an arrow deep infixed
> My panting side was charged, when I withdrew
> To seek a tranquil death in distant shades.
> There was I found by one who had himself
> Been hurt by the archers. In his side he bore
> And in his hands and feet the cruel scars,
> With gentle force soliciting the darts,
> He drew them forth and healed and bade me live.

The long-sought fountain is found! The light
has shone upon the road that leads him to the Lamb!

XIII

DAVID LIVINGSTONE'S TEXT

I

'*IT is the word of a gentleman of the most strict and sacred honour, so there's an end of it!*' says Livingstone to himself as he places his finger for the thousandth time on the text on which he stakes his life. He is surrounded by hostile and infuriated savages. During the sixteen years that he has spent in Africa, he has never before seemed in such imminent peril. Death stares him in the face. He thinks sadly of his life-work scarcely begun. For the first time in his experience he is tempted to steal away under cover of the darkness and to seek safety in flight. He prays! 'Leave me not, forsake me not!' he cries. But let me quote from his own journal: it will give us the rest of the story.

'*January* 14, 1856 *Evening*. Felt much turmoil of spirit in prospect of having all my plans for the welfare of this great region and this teeming population knocked on the head by savages to-morrow. But I read that Jesus said: "All power is given unto Me in heaven and in earth. Go ye therefore, and teach all nations, and *lo, I am with you alway, even unto the end of the world.*" It is the word of a gentleman of the most strict and sacred honour,

so there's an end of it! I will not cross furtively
to-night as I intended. Should such a man as I
flee? Nay, verily, I shall take observations for lati-
tude and longitude to-night, though they may be the
last. I feel quite calm now, thank God!'

The words in italics are underlined in the journal,
and they were underlined in his heart. Later in the
same year, he pays his first visit to the Homeland
Honours are everywhere heaped upon him. The
University of Glasgow confers upon him the degree
of Doctor of Laws. On such occasions the recipient
of the honour is usually subjected to some banter
at the hands of the students. But when Livingstone
rises, bearing upon his person the marks of his strug-
gles and sufferings in darkest Africa, he is received
in reverential silence. He is gaunt and haggard as
a result of his long exposure to the tropical sun. On
nearly thirty occasions he has been laid low by the
fevers that steam from the inland swamps, and these
severe illnesses have left their mark His left arm,
crushed by the lion, hangs helplessly at his side. A
hush falls upon the great assembly as he announces
his resolve to return to the land for which he has
already endured so much. 'But I return,' he says,
'without misgiving and with great gladness. For
would you like me to tell you what supported me
through all the years of exile among people whose
language I could not understand, and whose attitude towards me was always uncertain and often
hostile? It was this: *"Lo, I am with you alway,*

even unto the end of the world!" On those words I staked everything, and they never failed!'

'Leave me not, forsake me not!' he prays.

'Lo, I am with you alway, even unto the end of the world!' comes the response.

'It is the word of a gentleman of the most strict and sacred honour, so there's an end of it!' he tells himself.

On that pledge he hazarded his all. And it did not fail him.

II

When, I wonder, did David Livingstone first make that text his own? I do not know. It must have been very early. He used to say that he never had any difficulty in carrying with him his father's portrait because, in 'The Cottar's Saturday Night,' Robert Burns had painted it for him. Down to the last morning that he spent in his old home at Blantyre, the household joined in family worship. It was still dark when they knelt down that bleak November morning. They are up at five. The mother makes the coffee: the father prepares to walk with his boy to Glasgow; and David himself leads the household to the Throne of Grace. The thought embedded in his text is uppermost in his mind. He is leaving those who are dearer to him than life itself; yet there is One on whose Presence he can still rely. *'Lo, I am with you alway, even unto the end of the world.'* And so, in selecting the

passage to be read by lamplight in the little kitchen
on this memorable morning, David selects the Psalm
that, more clearly than any other, promises him, on
every sea and on every shore, the Presence of his
Lord. *'The Lord is thy keeper. The sun shall not
smite thee by day, nor the moon by night. The Lord
shall preserve thee from all evil: He shall preserve
thy soul. The Lord shall preserve thy going out
and thy coming in from this time forth, and even for
evermore.'* After prayers comes the anguish of farewell. But the ordeal is softened for them all by the
thought that has been suggested by David's reading
and by David's prayer. In the grey light of that
wintry morning, father and son set out on their
long and cheerless tramp. I remember, years ago,
standing on the Broomielow, on the spot that witnessed their parting. I could picture the elder man
turning sadly back towards his Lanarkshire home,
whilst David hurried off to make his final preparations for sailing. But, deeper than their sorrow,
there is in each of their hearts a song—the song of
the Psalm they have read together in the kitchen—
the song of the Presence—the song of the text!

'Leave me not, forsake me not!' cries the lonely
lad.

*'Lo, I am with you alway, even unto the end of
the world!'*

*'It is the word of a gentleman of the most strict
and sacred honour, so there's an end of it!'*   ·

And with that song singing itself in his soul,

David Livingstone turns his face towards darkest Africa.

III

If ever a man needed a comrade, David Livingstone did. Apart from that divine companionship, his is the most lonely life in history. It is doubtless good for the world that most men are content to marry and settle down, to weave about themselves the web of domestic felicity, to face each day the task that lies nearest to them, and to work out their destiny without worrying about the remote and the unexplored. But it is equally good for the world that there are a few adventurous spirits in every age who feel themselves taunted and challenged and dared by the mystery of the great unknown. As long as there is a pole undiscovered, a sea uncharted, a forest untracked or a desert uncrossed, they are restless and ill at ease. It is the most sublime form that curiosity assumes. From the moment of his landing on African soil, Livingstone is haunted, night and day, by the visions that beckon and the voices that call from out of the undiscovered. For his poor wife's sake he tries hard, and tries repeatedly, to settle down to the life of an ordinary mission station. But it is impossible. The lure of the wilds fascinates him. He sees, away on the horizon, the smoke of a thousand native settlements in which no white man has ever been seen. It is more than he can bear. He goes to some of them

and beholds, on arrival, the smoke of yet other settlements still further away.   And so he wanders
further and further from his starting point; and
builds home after home, only to desert each home as
soon as it is built!   The tales that the natives tell
him of vast inland seas and of wild tumultuous
waters tantalise him beyond endurance.   The in-
stincts of the hydrographer tingle within him.   He
sees the three great rivers—the Nile, the Congo and
the Zambesi—emptying themselves into three separate oceans, and he convinces himself that the man
who can solve the riddle of their sources will have
opened up a continent to the commerce and civilisation of the world.   The treasures of history present us with few things more affecting than the
hold that this ambition secures upon his heart.   It
lures him on and on—along the tortuous slavetracks
littered everywhere with bones—through the long
grass that stands up like a wall on either side of him
—across the swamps, the marshes and the bogs of
the watersheds—through forests dark as night and
through deserts that no man has ever crossed before
—on and on for more than thirty thousand miles.
He makes a score of discoveries, any one of which
would have established his fame; but none of these
satisfy him.   The unknown still calls loudly and will
not be denied.   Even at the last, worn to a shadow,
suffering in every limb, and too feeble to put his
feet to the ground, the mysterious fountains of
Herodotus torture his fancy.   'The fountains!' he

murmurs in his delirium, 'the hidden fountains!'
And with death stamped upon his face, he orders
his faithful blacks to bear him on a rude litter in
his tireless search for the elusive streams. Yet never
once does he feel really lonely. One has but to read
his journal in order to see that that word of stainless
honour never failed him. The song that soothed
and comforted the weeping household in the Blantyre kitchen cheered with its music the hazards and
adventures of his life in Africa.

'*Leave me not, forsake me not!*'

'*Lo, I am with you alway, even unto the end of
the world!*'

'*It is the word of a gentleman of the most strict
and sacred honour, so there's an end of it!*'

Thus, amidst savages and solitudes, Livingstone
finds that great word grandly true.

IV

'*It is His word of honour!*' says Livingstone; and,
nothing if not practical, he straightway proceeds to
act upon it. 'If He be with me, I can do anything,
anything, anything!' It is the echo of another
apostolic boast: 'I can do all things through Christ
that strengtheneth me!' In that unwavering confidence, and with an audacity that is the best evidence
of his faith, Livingstone draws up for himself a
programme so colossal that it would still have
seemed large had it been the project of a million
men. '*It is His word of honour!*' he reasons; 'and if

He will indeed be with me, even unto the end, He and I can accomplish what a million men, unattended by the Divine Companion, would tremble to attempt.' And so he draws up with a calm hand and a fearless heart that prodigious programme from which he never for a moment swerved, and which, when all was over, was inscribed upon his tomb in Westminster Abbey. Relying on 'the word of a gentleman of the most strict and sacred honour,' he sets himself—

1. *To evangelise the native races.*
2. *To explore the undiscovered secrets.*
3. *To abolish the desolating slave-trade.*

Some men set themselves to evangelise; some make it their business to explore; others feel called to emancipate; but Livingstone, with a golden secret locked up in his heart, undertakes all three!

Evangelisation!
Exploration!
Emancipation!

Those were his watchwords. No man ever set himself a more tremendous task: no man ever confronted his lifework with a more serene and joyous confidence!

V

And how did it all work out? Was his faith justified? Was that *word of honour* strictly kept?

'*Leave me not, forsake me not!*' he cries.

'*Lo, I am with you alway, even unto the end!*'

In spite of that assurance, did he ever find himself a solitary in a strange and savage land? Was he ever left or forsaken? It sometimes looked like it.

It looked like it when he stood, bent with anguish beside that sad and lonely grave at Shupanga. Poor Mary Livingstone—the daughter of Robert and Mary Moffat—was never strong enough to be the constant companion of a pioneer. For years she struggled on through dusty deserts and trackless jungles seeing no other woman but the wild women about her. But, with little children at her skirts, she could not struggle on for long. She gave it up, and stayed at home to care for the bairns and to pray for her husband as he pressed tirelessly on. But, even in Africa, people will talk. The gossips at the white settlements were incapable of comprehending any motive that could lead a man to leave his wife and plunge into the interior, save the desire to be as far from her as possible. Hearing of the scandal, and stung by it, Livingstone, in a weak moment, sent for his wife to again join him. She came; she sickened; and she died. We have all been touched by that sad scene in the vast African solitude. We seem to have seen him sitting beside the rude bed, formed of boxes covered with a soft mattress, on which lies his dying wife. The man who has faced so many deaths, and braved so many dangers, is now utterly broken down. He weeps like a child. 'Oh, my Mary, my Mary!' he cries, as the gentle spirit sighs itself away, 'I loved you when I married you, and, the longer I lived with you, I loved you the more! How often we have longed for a quiet home since you and I were cast adrift in Africa! God pity the poor children!' He buries her under the large baobab-tree, sixty feet in circumference, and reverently marks her grave. 'For the first time in my life,' he says, 'I feel willing to die! I am left alone in the world by one whom I felt to be a part of myself!'

'Leave me not, forsake me not!' he cried at the outset.

'I am left alone!' he cries in his anguish now.

Has the *word of honour* been violated? Has it? It certainly looks like it!

VI

It looked like it, too, eleven years later, when his own time came. He is away up among the bogs and the marshes near Chitambo's village in Ilala. Save only for his native helpers, he is all alone. He is all alone, and at the end of everything. He walked as long as he could walk; rode as long as he could ride; and was carried on a litter as long as he could bear it. But now, with his feet too ulcerated to bear the touch of the ground; with his frame so emaciated that it frightens him when he sees it in the glass; and with the horrible inward hemorrhage draining away his scanty remnant of vitality, he can go no further. 'Knocked up quite!' he says, in the last

indistinct entry in his journal. A drizzling rain is
falling, and the black men hastily build a hut to
shelter him. In his fever, he babbles about the fountains, the sources of the rivers, the undiscovered
streams. Two of the black boys, almost as tired as
their master, go to rest, appointing a third to watch
the sick man's bed. But he, too, sleeps. And when
he wakes, in the cold grey of the dawn, the vision
that confronts him fills him with terror. The white
man is not in bed, but on his knees beside it! He
runs and awakens his two companions. They creep
timidly to the kneeling figure. It is cold and stiff!
Their great master is dead! No white man near!
No woman's hand to close his eyes in that last cruel
sickness! No comrade to fortify his faith with the
deathless words of everlasting comfort and everlasting hope! He dies alone!

'Leave me not; forsake me not!' he cried at the
beginning.

'He died alone!'—that is how it all ended!

Has the *word of honour* been violated? It most
certainly looks like it!

VII

But it only *looks* like it! Life is full of illusions,
and so is death. Anyone who cares to read the
records in the journal of that terrible experience
at Shupanga will be made to feel that never for a
moment did *the word of honour* really fail.

'Lo, I am with you alway, even unto the end!'

The consciousness of that unfailing Presence was his one source of comfort as he sat by his wife's bedside and dug her grave. The assurance of that divine Presence was the one heartening inspiration that enabled him to take up his heavy burden and struggle on again!

'Lo, I am with you alway, even unto the end!'

Yes, even unto the end! Take just one more peep at the scene in the hut at Chitambo's village. He died on his knees! Then to whom was he talking when he died? He was talking even to the last moment of his life, to the constant Companion of his long, long pilgrimage! He was speaking, even in the act and article of death, to that 'Gentleman of the most strict and sacred honour' whose word he had so implicitly trusted.

'He will keep His word'—it is among the last entries in his journal—'He will keep His word, the Gracious One, full of grace and truth; no doubt of it. He will keep His word, and it will be all right. Doubt is here inadmissible, surely!'

'Leave me not; forsake me not!' he cried at the beginning.

'Lo, I am with you alway, even unto the end!' came the assuring response.

'It is the word of a gentleman of the most strict and sacred honour, so there's an end of it!'

And that pathetic figure on his knees is the best testimony to the way in which that sacred pledge was kept.

XIV

C. H. SPURGEON'S TEXT

I

Snow! Snow! Snow!

It was the first Sunday of the New Year, and this was how it opened! On roads and footpaths the snow was already many inches deep; the fields were a sheet of blinding whiteness; and the flakes were still falling as though they never meant to stop. As the caretaker fought his way through the storm from his cottage to the chapel in Artillery Street, he wondered whether, on such a wild and wintry day, anyone would venture out. It would be strange if, on the very first Sunday morning of the year, there should be no service. He unbolted the chapel doors and lit the furnace under the stove. Half an hour later, two men were seen bravely trudging their way through the snowdrifts; and, as they stood on the chapel steps, their faces flushed with their recent exertions, they laughingly shook the snow from off their hats and overcoats. What a morning, to be sure! By eleven o'clock about a dozen others had arrived; but where was the minister? They waited; but he did not come. He lived at a distance, and, in all probability, had found the roads impassable. What was to be done? The stewards looked at each other and surveyed the congregation. Except for a boy of fifteen sitting under the gallery, every face was known to them, and the range of selection was not great. There were whisperings and hasty consultations, and at last one of the two men who were first to arrive—'a poor, thin-looking man, a shoemaker, a tailor, or something of that sort'—yielded to the murmured entreaties of the others and mounted the pulpit steps. He glanced nervously round upon nearly three hundred empty seats. Nearly, but not quite! For there were a dozen or fifteen of the regular worshippers present, and there was the boy sitting under the gallery. People who had braved such a morning deserved all the help that he could give them, and the strange boy under the gallery ought not to be sent back into the storm feeling that there was nothing in the service for him. And so the preacher determined to make the most of his opportunity; and he did.

The boy sitting under the gallery! A marble tablet now adorns the wall near the seat which he occupied that snowy day. The inscription records that, that very morning, the boy sitting under the gallery was converted! He was only fifteen, and he died at fifty-seven. But, in the course of the intervening years, he preached the gospel to millions and led thousands and thousands into the kingdom and service of Jesus Christ. 'Let preachers study this story!' says Sir William Robertson Nicoll. 'Let them believe that, under the most adverse circum-

stances, they may do a work that will tell on the
universe for ever. It was a great thing to have converted Charles Haddon Spurgeon; and who knows
but he may have in the smallest and humblest congregation in the world some lad as well worth con-
verting as was he?'

II

Snow! Snow! Snow!

The boy sitting under the gallery had purposed
attending quite another place of worship that Sunday morning. No thought of the little chapel in
Artillery Street occurred to him as he strode out
into the storm. Not that he was very particular.
Ever since he was ten years of age he had felt
restless and ill at ease whenever his mind turned to
the things that are unseen and eternal. 'I had been
about five years in the most fearful distress of mind,'
he says. 'I thought the sun was blotted out of my
sky, that I had so sinned against God that there was
no hope for me!' He prayed, but never had a
glimpse of an answer. He attended every place of
worship in the town; but no man had a message
for a youth who only wanted to know what he must
do to be saved. With the first Sunday of the New
Year he purposed yet another of these ecclesiastical
experiments. But in making his plans he had not
reckoned on the ferocity of the storm. 'I sometimes think,' he said, years afterwards, 'I sometimes think I might have been in darkness and

despair now, had it not been for the goodness of God in sending a snowstorm on Sunday morning, January 6th, 1850, when I was going to a place of worship. When I could go no further I turned down a court and came to a little Primitive Methodist chapel.' Thus the strange boy sitting under the gallery came to be seen by the impromptu speaker that snowy morning! Thus, as so often happens, a broken programme pointed the path of destiny! Who says that two wrongs can never make a right? Let them look at this! The plans at the chapel went wrong; the minister was snowed up. The plans of the boy under the gallery went wrong: the snowstorm shut him off from the church of his choice. Those two wrongs together made one tremendous right; for out of those shattered plans and programmes came an event that has incalculably enriched mankind.

III

Snow! Snow! Snow!

And the very snow seemed to mock his misery. It taunted him as he walked to church that morning. Each virgin snowflake as it fluttered before his face and fell at his feet only emphasised the dreadful pollution within. 'My original and inward pollution!' he cries with Bunyan; 'I was more loathsome in mine own eyes than a toad. Sin and corruption would as naturally bubble out of my heart as water out of a fountain. I thought that every one had a better heart than I had. At the sight of my own vileness I fell deeply into despair.' These words of Bunyan's exactly reflect, he tells us, his own secret and spiritual history. And the white, white snow only intensified the agonising consciousness of defilement. In the expressive phraseology of the Church of England Communion Service, 'the remembrance of his sins was grievous unto him; the burden of them was intolerable.' 'I counted the estate of everything that God had made far better than this dreadful state of mind was: yea, gladly would I have been in the condition of a dog or a horse; for I knew they had no souls to perish under the weight of sin as mine was like to do.' 'Many and many a time,' says Mr. Thomas Spurgeon, 'my father told me that, in those early days, he was so stormtossed and distressed by reason of his sins that he found himself envying the very beasts in the field and the toads by the wayside!' So stormtossed! The storm that raged around him that January morning was in perfect keeping with the storm within; but oh, for the whiteness, the pure, unsullied whiteness, of the falling snow!

IV

Snow! Snow! Snow!

From out of that taunting panorama of purity the boy passed into the cavernous gloom of the almost empty building. Its leaden heaviness matched the mood of his spirit, and he stole furtively to a seat under the gallery. He noticed the long pause; the anxious glances which the stewards exchanged with each other; and, a little later, the whispered consultations. He watched curiously as the hastily-appointed preacher—'a shoemaker or something of that sort'—awkwardly ascended the pulpit. 'The man was,' Mr. Spurgeon tells us, 'really stupid as you would say. He was obliged to stick to his text for the simple reason that he had nothing else to say. His text was, *"Look unto Me and be ye saved, all the ends of the earth."* He did not even pronounce the words rightly, but that did not matter. There was, I thought, a glimpse of hope for me in the text, and I listened as though my life depended upon what I heard. In about ten minutes the preacher had got to the end of his tether. Then he saw me sitting under the gallery; and I daresay, with so few present, he knew me to be a stranger. He then said: "Young man, you look very miserable." Well, I did; but I had not been accustomed to have remarks made from the pulpit on my personal appearance. However, it was a good blow, well struck. He continued: "And you will always be miserable—miserable in life, and miserable in death—if you do not obey my text. But if you obey now, this moment, you will be saved!" Then he shouted, as only a Primitive Methodist can shout, "Young man, look to Jesus! look, look, *look!*" I did; and, then and there, the cloud was gone, the darkness had rolled away, and that moment I saw

the sun! I could have risen on the instant and sung
with the most enthusiastic of them of the precious
blood of Christ and of the simple faith which looks
alone to Him. Oh, that somebody had told me before! In their own earnest way, they sang a Hallelujah before they went home, and I joined in it!'

The snow around!

The defilement within!

*'Look unto Me and be ye saved, all the ends of
the earth!'*

'Precious blood . . . and simple faith!'

'I sang a Hallelujah!'

V

Snow! Snow! Snow!

The snow was falling as fast as ever when the
boy sitting under the gallery rose and left the
building. The storm raged just as fiercely. And
yet the snow was not the same snow! Everything
was changed. Mr. Moody has told us that, on the
day of his conversion, all the birds in the hedgerow
seemed to be singing newer and blither songs. Dr.
Campbell Morgan declares that the very leaves on
the trees appeared to him more beautiful on the day
that witnessed the greatest spiritual crisis in his
career. Frank Bullen was led to Christ in a little
New Zealand port which I have often visited, by a
worker whom I knew well. And he used to say that,
next morning, he climbed the summit of a mountain

near by and the whole landscape seemed changed.
Everything had been transformed in the night!

> Heaven above is softer blue,
>   Earth around a deeper green,
> Something lives in every hue
>   Christless eyes have never seen.
>
> Birds with gladder songs o'erflow,
>   Flowers with richer beauties shine,
> Since I know, as now I know,
>   I am His and He is mine!

'I was now so taken with the love of God,' says
Bunyan—and here again Mr. Spurgeon says that
the words might have been his own—'I was now so
taken with the love and mercy of God that I could
not tell how to contain till I got home. I thought I
could have spoken of His love, and told of His
mercy, even to the very crows that sat upon the
ploughed lands before me, had they been capable
of understanding me.' As the boy from under the
gallery walked home that morning he laughed at the
storm, and the snow that had mocked him coming
sang to him as he returned. 'The snow was lying
deep,' he says, 'and more was falling But those
words of David kept ringing through my heart,
"Wash me, and I shall be whiter than snow!" It
seemed to me as if all Nature was in accord with
the blessed deliverance from sin which I had found
in a moment by looking to Jesus Christ!'

The mockery of the snow!
The text amidst the snow!
The music of the snow!

Whiter than the snow!
'Look unto Me and be ye saved!'
'Wash me, and I shall be whiter than snow!'

VI

'Look unto Me and be ye saved!'
Look! Look! Look!

I look to my doctor to heal me when I am hurt; I look to my lawyer to advise me when I am perplexed; I look to my tradesmen to bring my daily supplies to my door; but there is only One to whom I can look when my soul cries out for deliverance.

'Look unto Me and be ye saved, all the ends of the earth!'

'Look! Look! Look!' cried the preacher.

'I looked,' says Mr. Spurgeon, 'until I could almost have looked my eyes away; and in heaven I will look still, in joy unutterable!'

Happy the preacher, however unlettered, who, knowing little else, knows how to direct such wistful and hungry eyes to the only possible fountain of satisfaction!

XV

DEAN STANLEY'S TEXT

I

TOWARDS the close of his 'Life of Dean Stanley,' Mr. Prothero tells a capital story. A gentleman, travelling from Norwich to Liverpool, entered a third-class smoking compartment and was soon absorbed in conversation with a couple of soldiers whom he found there. The gentleman's confession that he came from Norwich suggested to the soldiers the name of Dean Stanley, who lived in that city. The gentleman asked what *they* knew about Dean Stanley.

'Oh,' replied one of them, 'me and my mate here have cause to bless the Lord that we ever saw good Dean Stanley, sir, I can tell you!'

They went on to explain that they once had a day in London. They were anxious to see all the sights, but, by the time they reached Westminster Abbey, the doors were being closed for the night. Extremely disappointed, they were turning sadly away when a gentleman approached and asked if they could not return on the morrow. The soldiers explained that it was impossible. The gentleman, who proved to be the Dean, thereupon took the keys from the beadle, and himself showed them every

part of the Abbey. As he prepared to take leave of
them he commented upon the grandeur of being immortalised by a monument in Westminster Abbey.
'But, after all,' he added, 'you may both have a more
enduring monument than this, for this will moulder
into dust and be forgotten, but *you,* if your names
are written in *the Lamb's Book of Life, you* will
abide for ever!' He invited them to breakfast next
morning, and insisted on paying their fares to their
homes, and again, in bidding them good-bye, urged
them to be sure to see that their names were written
in *the Lamb's Book of Life,* 'and then,' he added,
'if we never meet again on earth, we shall certainly
meet in heaven!'

'And so we parted with the Dean,' said the soldier, in concluding his story in the train, 'and as
we travelled home we talked about our visit to the
Abbey, and puzzled much as to the meaning of the
Lamb's Book of Life!'

'It will be enough to say,' observes Mr. Prothero,
in placing the story on record, 'it will be enough to
say that those words proved the turning point in the
lives of those two men and of their wives, and that,
as one of them said, "We trust that our names are
written in *the Lamb's Book of Life,* and that we
may some day, in God's good time, meet Dean Stanley in heaven!"'

The Lamb!
The Lamb's Book!
The Lamb's Book of Life!

'And there shall in no wise enter into the city anything that defileth, neither whatsoever worketh abomination or maketh a lie, but they which are written in *the Lamb's Book of Life!*'

II

God is a great believer in putting things down. 'I looked,' says John, 'and, behold, I saw the *books;* and the *books* were opened; and *another book* was opened, which is the *Book of Life,* and the dead were judged out of those things which were written in *the books.*' John saw books everywhere. It is the books, the books, the books! In the old slave days in America, the darkeys on the cotton plantations used to make their owners tremble by the zest with which, at their camp meetings, they shouted a certain chorus:

> My Lord sees all you do,
> And my Lord hears all you say,
> And my Lord keep a-writing all the time!

It was a Western appropriation of an Eastern revelation. The slaves gloried in the highly-coloured imagery of the Apocalypse. No book was so dear to them as the book with which the Bible closes. And when they read about the books, God's books, the books that hold the evidence, the books that must all be opened, they sang for very joy. The slaves shouted and the owners shuddered; the books, the books, the books! God puts things down!

III

He writes everywhere and on everything. He
is the most voluminous author in the universe.
Every leaf in the forest, every sand on the seashore,
is smothered with his handwriting. The trouble is
that I am so slow to recognise the manuscripts of
God. I walk past a tree, and to me it is only a tree—
a leafy elm, a tasselled birch, a flowery chestnut, a
rustling plane or a spreading oak. But a man whose
eyes have been opened will find in the tree a volume
of autobiography. Its history is written in its tissue.
A practised eye can tell at a glance how long it has
stood here; and can read, as from the pages of a
book, the story of the tree's experiences. The winds
by which it has been buffeted; the accidents that have
befallen it; the diseases from which it has suffered;
the way in which it has been nurtured or starved by
congenial or uncongenial soil; it is all written down.
A botanist could open the book and interpret the entire romance.

I stand and watch men dig a well. The windlass
revolves; the great buckets go down empty and
come up full; the earth is thrown on to the heap;
and the process is repeated. I see this, and I see
no more. But a geologist would tell me that these
men are digging amongst ancient libraries. Every
clod is a record; every stone a sign. Standing here
at the mouth of the well, with his glass in one hand
and his hammer in the other, he would pounce upon

this and would probe into that, and would tell a
most wonderful tale. To him these are the archives
of antiquity. They tell him of floods and tornadoes
and earthquakes of which no other records survive.
He taps at a stone, and crumbles a lump of loam,
and straightway tells you of the flora and fauna of
the district in some prehistoric time. It is all written down; nothing happens without leaving its
record. God is a great believer in bookkeeping.

No man can walk down the street by night or by
day without placing on record the story of his movements. My senses may be too dull to trace him;
but call out the black trackers or the bloodhounds,
and they will soon convince you that every footstep
was like a signature. Read a great detective story,
and it will soon occur to you that your Sherlock
Holmes proceeds on the assumption that every secret
thing is recorded somewhere and somehow: the only
trouble is to lay your hand on the exact volume and
correctly decipher its mysterious hieroglyphics. It
is to that task that the detective dedicates his skill.
The whole science of finger-print evidence shows that
I cannot touch a stick or straw in the solar system
without leaving a record of my act, signed and
sealed, upon the spot.

IV

History is written automatically. It is wonderful
what you find when you are moving. The Autocrat
of the Breakfast Table, engaged one day on some

such domestic upheaval, stumbled upon this very
truth. He found it behind a set of bookshelves.
'There is nothing that happens,' he says, in telling
the story, 'which must not inevitably, and which
does not actually, photograph itself in every con-
ceivable aspect and in all dimensions. The infinite
galleries of the Past await but one brief process,
and all their pictures will be called out and fixed for
ever. We had a curious illustration of this great
fact on a very humble scale. When a certain bookcase, long standing in one place, for which it was
built, was removed, there was the exact image on
the wall of the whole, and of many of its portions.
But in the midst of this picture was another—the
precise outline of a map which had hung on the wall
before the bookcase was built. We had all forgotten everything about the map until we saw its photograph on the wall. Then we remembered it, as
some day or other we may remember a sin which
has been built over and covered up, when this lower
universe is pulled away from before the wall of
Infinity where the wrongdoing stands self-recorded.'
One of the old Hebrew prophets declared that the
sin of Judah is written with a pen of iron. Everything is! my doings are dotted down. Even if
they are written nowhere else, they are entered
upon the tablets of my memory. Often the character reflects itself in the countenance. Life's story is
variously and indelibly inscribed. There are books,
books, books; books everywhere; the universe itself

is but a massive volume beautifully bound. It takes a lot of reading, but God can make out every word.

V

The books! The books!
The dead were judged out of the books!
What does it mean?

It means that the judgements of God are *terribly deliberate*. I shall never forget an impression made upon my mind in my early boyhood. Father woke me early in the morning. He was going to London : would I care to go with him? Those were always my red-letter days. The trip and the business in hand occupied most of the morning, and then we were free. Where should we go? Now it happened that I was very fond of reading the reports of famous trials. I thought that actually to witness one would be a most exciting experience Accordingly, I asked to be taken to the law courts. Shall I ever forget the bitter disillusionment? I saw the judge seated upon his bench; I saw the barristers, the witnesses and all the principal parties to the suit. But the proceedings themselves! I heard a barrister ask a question, the sense of which I could with difficulty distinguish. I heard a mumbled reply, but failed to catch the words uttered. I saw the judge bend over his desk and carefully write something down. Another question : another inaudible reply : another pause whilst the judge entered something in his book. I came away disgusted. My boyish

dream was shattered. Yet somehow the years have
dispelled the disappointment. I like now to think
of justice as calm, passionless, deliberate. The
judge is unswayed by caprice, vindictiveness or
wrath. He is terribly deliberate. He writes everything down. He judges according to the things that
appear *in the books*.

It means, too, that the judgements of God are
scrupulously accurate. 'I looked, and, behold, I
saw *the books!*' I ask my tradesman how much I
owe him. He scratches his head, hums and ha's
for a minute, and then tells me that it comes to ten
and sixpence. I pay him grudgingly, feeling that
the position is very unsatisfactory. Again, I ask
my tradesman how much I owe him. He reaches
down a ledger, opens it, and tells me that I owe him
ten and sixpence. I pay him cheerfully. His ac-
curacy gives me confidence. *The books* make all
the difference.

It means, too, that the judgements of God are
wonderfully comprehensive and complete. Dean
Stanley, who loved the old Abbey so well, never
wandered through transept, aisle or nave without
feeling, as he gazed upon its stately marbles, that
the judgement of humanity is far from satisfactory.
Many names are immortalised in the Abbey that
might well be permitted to perish : many who served
their country nobly find no memorial there. The
scroll of fame is incomplete. He loved, therefore,
to ponder on another scroll that should be disfigured

by no such blemishes. 'See to it,' he used to say, 'that your name is written, not in marble that must crumble, but in *the Lamb's Book of Life!*'

VI

I am glad that that *'other book'* that John saw opened was the Book of *Life*. Westminster Abbey enshrines the names of the illustrious *dead:* that other book—the last and the best that John saw opened—contains only the names of those who are *alive*—and *alive for evermore.* 'I am come that ye might have *life,'* said Jesus, in one of His historic manifestoes, 'I am come that ye might have *life,* and that ye might have it more abundantly.' 'For God so loved the world that He gave His only be-gotten Son that whosoever believeth in Him should not perish but have *everlasting life.'* The Saviour is the *Fountain of Life;* the Gospel is a *Message of Life,* the Volume that John saw opened in heaven was the *Book of Life.* There is infinite comfort in that.

I am glad, too, that it is the *Lamb's* book. My heart would fail me if that awful volume had been inscribed by any hand but His. Lachlan Campbell was a good man; he was the strictest and the stern-est of the elders of Drumtochty; and he loved Flora, his erring daughter, dearly. But he was over-hasty in striking her name out of the family Bible. We all remember the rebuke that Marget Howe administered to him, when she saw the book, its ink all blurred by tears.

'This is what ye hev dune,' she cried, 'and ye let a woman see yir wark. Ye are an auld man, and in sore travail, but a' tell ye before God, ye hae the greater shame. Juist twenty years o' age this spring, and her mither dead. Nae woman to watch over her, and she wandered frae the fold, and a' ye can dae is to take her oot o' yir Bible! Wae's me if oor Father had blotted oor names frae *the Book o' Life* when we left His hoose. But He sent His ain Son to seek us, an' a weary road He cam. Puir Flora, tae hae sic a father!'

Thanks to Marget's gracious intervention, Flora came home again; she was welcomed with endless tears and caresses; the Gaelic—'the best of all languages for loving'—contains fifty words for darling, and Lachlan used them all that night! The name had to be re-entered in the Bible, and Lachlan had to ask Flora's forgiveness for erasing it. I am glad that the book on which my eternal destiny depends is the *Lamb's* Book—*the Lamb's Book of Life!*

VII

Thackeray tells us that when good old Colonel Newcome—the greatest gentleman in literature—lay dying, the watchers noticed that his mind was moving backwards across the pageant of the years. He is in India addressing his regiment on parade! He is in Paris, living through the days of auld lang syne! And then! 'At the usual evening hour the chapel bell began to toll, and Thomas Newcome's hands outside the bed feebly beat time. And, just as the last bell struck, a peculiar sweet smile shone over his face, and he lifted up his head a little, and quickly said *"Adsum!"* and fell back. It was the word we used at school, when names were called; and lo, he whose heart was as that of a little child, had answered to his name, and stood in the presence of The Master!'

The Book!

The Lamb's Book!

The Lamb's Book of Life!

When that last volume is opened, and that last roll called, may I, like Colonel Newcome, be ready to answer gladly to my name!

XVI

WILLIAM CAREY'S TEXT

I

THE westering sun, slanting through the tops of the
taller trees, is beginning to throw long shadows
across the green and gently-undulating fields. The
brindled cattle, lying at their ease and meditatively
chewing the cud in these quiet Northamptonshire
pastures, are disturbed by the sound of footsteps
in the lane. Some of them rise in protest and stare
fixedly at the quaint figure that has broken so rudely
on their afternoon reverie. But he causes them no
alarm, for they have often seen him pass this way
before. He is the village cobbler. This very morning he tramped along his winding thoroughfare on
his way to Northampton. He was carrying his
wallet of shoes—a fortnight's work—to the Government contractor there. And now he is trudging
his way back to Moulton with the roll of leather
that will keep him busy for another week or two.
The cattle stare at him, as well they may. The
whole world would stare at him if it had the chance
to-day. For this is William Carey, the harbinger
of a new order, the prophet of a new age, the maker
of a new world! The cattle stare at him, but he

has no eyes for them. His thoughts are over the seas and far away. He is a dreamer; but he is a dreamer who means business. Less than twenty years ago, in a tall chestnut tree not far from this very lane, he spied a bird's nest that he greatly coveted. He climbed—and fell! He climbed again —and fell again! He climbed a third time, and, in the third fall, broke his leg. A few weeks later, whilst the limb was still bandaged, his mother left him for an hour or two, instructing him to take the greatest care of himself in her absence. When she returned, he was sitting in his chair, flushed and excited, *with the bird's nest on his knees.*

'Hurrah, mother; I've done it at last! Here it is, look!'

'You don't mean to tell me you've climbed that tree again!'

'I couldn't help it, mother; I couldn't, really! *If I begin a thing I must go through with it!'*

On monuments erected in honour of William Carey, on busts and plaques and pedestals, on the titlepages of his innumerable biographies, and under pictures that have been painted of him, I have often seen inscribed some stirring sentence that fell from his eloquent lips. But I have never seen that one. Yet the most characteristic word that Carey ever uttered was the reply that he made to his mother that day!

'If I begin a thing I must go through with it!'

If you look closely, you will see that sentence

stamped upon his countenance as, with a far-away look in his eye, he passes down the lane Let us follow him, and we shall find that he is beginning some tremendous things; and, depend upon it, he will at any cost go through with them!

II

It is not an elaborately-furnished abode, this little home of his. For, although he is minister, school-master and cobbler, the three vocations only provide him with about thirty-six pounds a year. Looking around, I can see but a few stools, his cobbler's out-fit, a book or two (including a Bible, a copy of Cap-tain Cook's Voyages and a Dutch Grammar) besides a queer-looking map on the wall. We must have a good look at this map, for there is history in it as well as geography. It is a map of the world, made of leather and brown paper, and it is the work of his own fingers. Look, I say, at this map, for it is a reflection of the soul of Carey. As he came up the lane, looking neither to the right hand nor to the left, he was thinking of the world. He is a jack-of-all-trades, yet he is a man of a single thought. 'Per-haps,' he says to himself, 'perhaps God means what He says!' The world! The world! *The World!* God so loved *the world!* Go ye into all *the world!* The kingdoms of *the world* shall become the king-doms of our God and of His Christ! It is always the world, the world, *the world*. That thought haunted the mind of Carey night and day. The

map of the world hung in his room, but it only
hung in his room because it already hung in his
heart. He thought of it, he dreamed of it, he
preached of it. And he was amazed that, when
he unburdened his soul to his brother-ministers,
or preached on that burning theme to his little
congregation, they listened with respectful interest
and close attention, yet *did nothing*. At length, on
May 31, 1792, Carey preached his great sermon,
the sermon that gave rise to our modern missionary movement, the sermon that made history. It
was at Nottingham. *'Lengthen thy cords'*—so ran
the text—*'lengthen thy cords and strengthen thy
stakes, for thou shalt break forth on the right hand
and on the left; and thy seed shall inherit the Gen-
tiles and make the desolate cities to be inhabited.'*

'Lengthen thy cords!' said the text.

'Strengthen thy stakes!' said the text.

'Expect great things from God!' said the preacher.

'Attempt great things for God!' said the preacher.

'If all the people had lifted up their voices and
wept,' says Dr. Ryland, 'as the children of Israel
did at Bochim, I should not have wondered at the
effect; it would only have seemed proportionate to
the cause; so clearly did Mr. Carey prove the
criminality of our supineness in the cause of God!'
But the people did not weep! They did not even
wait! They rose to leave as usual. When Carey,
stepping down from the pulpit, saw the people
quietly dispersing, he seized Andrew Fuller's hand

and wrung it in an agony of distress. 'Are we not going to *do anything!*' he demanded. 'Oh, Fuller, call them back, call them back! We dare not separate *without doing anything!*' As a result of that passionate entreaty, a missionary society was formed, and William Carey offered himself as the Society's first missionary.

'*If I begin a thing I must go through with it!*' he said, as a schoolboy.

'*We dare not separate without doing something!*' he cried, as a young minister.

'*Lengthen the cords! Strengthen the stakes!*'
'*Expect great things! Attempt great things!*'

III

I can never think of William Carey without thinking of Jane Conquest. In the little hamlet by the sea, poor Jane watched through the night beside the cot of her dying child. Then, suddenly, a light leapt in at the lattice, crimsoning every object in the room. It was a ship on fire, and no eyes but hers had seen it! Leaving her dying boy to the great Father's care, she trudged through the snow to the old church on the hill.

She crept through the narrow window and climbed the belfry stair,
And grasped the rope, sole cord of hope for the mariners in despair.
And the wild wind helped her bravely, and she wrought with an earnest will,
And the clamorous bell spake out right well to the hamlet under the hill.

And it roused the slumbering fishers, nor its warning task
    gave o'er
Till a hundred fleet and eager feet were hurrying to the
    shore;
And the lifeboat midst the breakers, with a brave and gallant
    few,
O'ercame each check and reached the wreck and saved the
    hapless crew

Upon the sensitive soul of William Carey there
broke the startling vision of a world in peril, and
he could find no sleep for his eyes nor slumber
for his eyelids until the whole church was up and
doing for the salvation of the perishing millions.
It has been finely said that when, towards the
close of the eighteenth century, it pleased God to
awaken from her slumbers a drowsy and lethargic
church, there rang out, from the belfry of the
ages, a clamorous and insistent alarm; and, in that
arousing hour, the hand upon the bellrope was the
hand of William Carey.

'We dare not separate without doing something!'
'Lengthen the cords! Strengthen the stakes!'
'Expect great things! Attempt great things!'
'Here am I; send me, send me!'

IV

Now the life of William Carey is both the out-
come and the exemplification of a stupendous principle. That principle was never better stated than
by the prophet from whose flaming lips Carey
borrowed his text. *'Thine eyes,'* said Isaiah, *'Thine
eyes shall see the King in His beauty: they shall*

behold the land that stretches very far off.' The
vision *kingly* stands related to the vision *continental;*
the revelation of the Lord leads to the revelation of
the limitless landscape. What was it that happened
one memorable day upon the road to Damascus? It
was simply this: Saul of Tarsus saw the King in
His beauty! And what happened as a natural and
inevitable consequence? There came into his life
the passion of the far horizon. All the narrowing
limits of Jewish prejudice and the cramping bonds
of Pharisaic superstition fell from him like the scales
that seemed to drop from his eyes. The world is
at his feet. Single-handed and alone, taking his
life in his hand, he storms the great centres of
civilisation, the capitals of proud empires, in the
name of Jesus Christ. No difficulty can daunt him;
no danger impede his splendid progress. He passes
from sea to sea, from island to island, from continent to continent. The hunger of the earth is in
his soul; there is no coast or colony to which he will
not go. He feels himself a debtor to Greek and to
barbarian, to bond and to free. He climbs mountains, fords rivers, crosses continents, bears stripes,
endures imprisonments, suffers shipwreck, courts
insult, and dares a thousand deaths out of the passion
of his heart to carry the message of hope to every
crevice and corner of the earth. A more thrilling
story of hazard, hardship, heroism and adventure
has never been written. On the road to Damascus
Paul saw the King in His beauty, and he spent the

remainder of his life in exploiting the limitless landscape that unrolled itself before him. The vision of
the *King* opened to his eyes the vision of the *continents.* In every age these two visions have always
gone side by side. In the *fourteenth* century, the
vision of the King broke upon the soul of John
Wickliffe. Instantly, there arose the Lollards,
scouring city, town and hamlet with the new evangel,
the representatives of the instinct of the far horizon.
The *fifteenth* century contains two tremendous
names. As soon as the world received the vision
kingly by means of Savonarola, it received the
vision *continental* by means of Christopher Columbus. In the *sixteenth* century, the same principle
holds. It is, on the one hand, the century of Martin
Luther, and, on the other, the century of Raleigh,
Drake, Hawkins, Frobisher, Grenville and the great
Elizabethan navigators. All the oceans of the world
became a snowstorm of white sails. The *seventeenth* century gave us, first the Puritans, and then
the sailing of the *Mayflower.* So we came to the
eighteenth century. And the *eighteenth* century is
essentially the century of John Wesley and of
William Carey. At Aldersgate Street the vision of
the King in His beauty dawned graciously upon the
soul of John Wesley. During the fifty years that
followed, that vision fell, through Wesley's instru-
mentality, upon the entire English people The
Methodist revival of the eighteenth century is one
of the most gladsome records in the history of

Europe. And then, John Wesley having impressed upon all men the vision of the *King,* William Carey arose to impress upon them the vision of the *Continents.*

'We must do something!' he cried.

'Lengthen the cords! Strengthen the stakes!'

'Expect great things! Attempt great things!'

'The King! The King! The Continents! The Continents!'

V

Having gazed upon these things, our eyes are the better fitted to appreciate the significance of the contents of the cobbler's room. There he sits at his last, the Bible from which he drew his text spread out before him, and a home-made map of the world upon the wall! There is no element of chance about that artless record. There is a subtle and inevitable connection between the two. In the *Bible* he saw the King in His beauty: on the *map* he caught glimpses of the far horizon. To him, the two were inseparable; and, moved by the Vision of the Lord which he caught in the one, and by the Vision of the limitless landscape which he caught in the other, he left his last and made history.

VI

'Lengthen the cords! Strengthen the stakes!'
'Expect great things! Attempt great things!'
'Do something! Do something!'

It was at Nottingham that Carey preached that
arousing sermon: it was in India that he practised
it. With the eye of a statesman and of a strategist
he saw that the best way of regaining the ground
that was being lost in Europe was to achieve new
conquests in Asia. History abounds in striking
coincidences; but, among them all, there is none
more suggestive than the fact that it was on November 11, 1793—the very day on which the French
revolutionists tore the Cross from Notre Dame,
smashed it on the streets, and abjured Christianity
—that William Carey sailed up the Hooghly,-landed
at Calcutta, and claimed a new continent for Christ!
And, like a statesman and a strategist, he settled
down to do in India the work to which he had challenged the church at home.

'*Lengthen the cords!*'

'*Strengthen the stakes!*'

He started an indigo factory; made himself the
master of a dozen languages; became Professor of
Bengali, Sanskrit and Mahratta at a salary of fifteen
hundred a year, all in order to engage more and still
more missionaries and to multiply the activities by
which the Kingdom of Christ might be set up in
India. His work of translation was a marvel in
itself.

'*If I begin a thing I must go through with it!*'
he said that day with the birds'-nest resting on
his lap.

'*Do something! Do something!*' he said in his

agony as he saw the people dispersing after his sermon.

And in India he did things. He toiled terribly. But he sent the gospel broadcast through the lengths and breadths of that vast land; built up the finest college in the Indian Empire; and gave the peoples the Word of God in their own tongue.

VII

Just before Carey died, Alexander Duff arrived in India. He was a young Highlander of four-and-twenty, tall and handsome, with flashing eye and quivering voice. Before setting out on his own life-work he went to see the man who had changed the face of the world. He reached the college on a sweltering day in July. 'There he beheld a little yellow old man in a white jacket, who tottered up to the visitor, received his greetings, and with outstretched hands, solemnly blessed him.' Each fell in love with the other. Carey, standing on the brink of the grave, rejoiced to see the handsome and cultured young Scotsman dedicating his life to the evangelisation and emancipation of India. Duff felt that the old man's benediction would cling to his work like a fragrance through all the great and epoch-making days ahead

Not long after Carey lay a-dying, and, to his great delight, Duff came to see him. The young Highlander told the veteran of his admiration and his love. In a whisper that was scarcely audible,

the dying man begged his visitor to pray with him
After he had complied, and taken a sad farewell
of the frail old man, he turned to go. On reaching
the door he fancied that he heard his name. He
turned and saw that Mr. Carey was beckoning him.

'Mr. Duff,' said the dying man, his earnestness
imparting a new vigour to his voice, 'Mr. Duff, you
have been speaking about Dr. Carey, Dr. Carey, Dr.
Carey! When I am gone, say nothing about Dr.
Carey—speak only of Dr. Carey's Saviour.'

Did I say that, when our little cobbler startled the
cattle in the Northamptonshire lane, he was thinking
only of the world, the world, *the world?* I was
wrong! He was thinking primarily of the Saviour,
the Saviour, *the Saviour*—the *Saviour* of the *World!*

And yet I was right; for the two visions are one
vision, the two thoughts one thought.

The King, the King, the King!

The Continents, the Continents, the Continents!

The Saviour, the Saviour, the Saviour!

The World, the World, the World!

As a lad, Carey caught the vision of *the King in
His beauty;* and, as an inevitable consequence, he
spent his life in the conquest of *the land that is
very far off.*

XVII

JAMES HANNINGTON'S TEXT

I

HE is a proud young English gentleman—wealthy, cultured, athletic; and the words smite him like a blow in the face.

'Not fit for the Kingdom of God!'
'Not fit for the Kingdom of God!'

Those who know him best would say that he is fit for anything; yet *these* are the stinging words that confront him in the crisis of his young career.

'Not fit for the Kingdom of God!'
'Not fit for the Kingdom of God!'

He is the kind of fellow upon whom you would bestow a second glance if it were your good fortune to meet him on the street. He is tall, lithe, handsome, and splendidly proportioned. He strikes you as having every nerve and sinew under perfect control His face is vigorous and arresting. Without seeming in the least degree self-assertive or pugnacious, it suggests boundless energy and dauntless resolution. His eyes are grey and full of mischief. His voice is resonant, impressive, commanding. His laugh is boisterous, contagious, unforgettable. Although still young, he has travelled widely; has visited the famous cities of the continent; and, in his own yacht, has navigated the waterways of Europe. He is just finishing his university career at Oxford. Come with me to his room at St. Mary's Hall; and, as you glance around its walls, the medley of objects that will meet the eye will furnish us with some index to his character. In the centre of everything is a portrait of his mother, a stately and beautiful lady, from whom he has inherited many of his noblest traits. Arranged around it are the bones of many curious monsters, and the crude but cunning weapons of barbarous peoples. In the corner stands a miscellaneous collection of riding-whips; whilst here, under the window, stands a tank, in which numbers of live fish disport themselves. For our gay young undergraduate is a naturalist; the woods and the waters have taken him into their confidence and have freely yielded up their secrets.

Here he is, then, standing on the threshold of destiny! He appears to be one of fortune's darlings. All that exceptional gifts, careful training, extensive travel, and the highest education can do for a man has been done for him. And yet, as he prepares to turn all these priceless advantages to some account, and to set his face seriously towards his lifework, these are the words that smite him in the face and stab him to the quick!

'Not fit for the Kingdom of God!'
'Not fit for the Kingdom of God!'

Like the rich young ruler whom he so strikingly

resembles, he turns away sorrowful. The gaiety of his spirit is clouded in gloom. *'Not fit for the Kingdom of God!'* What is it that, with all his charms and his accomplishments, he still lacks?

II

It is on the eve of his ordination that these cruel words rebuke him. For, in striving to equip himself for the useful life that he so earnestly desires, he he has by no means forgotten the loftiest claims of all. The fear of God is constantly before his eyes With all his fun and frolic, his passion for sport and his thirst for adventure, James Hannington is in reality a fervently religious youth. At the back of his mind he is revolving some tremendous problems. Let me copy a couple of entries from his private journal. The one was written in his eighteenth year; the other in his twentieth.

'*March* 20, 1868: I have been much tempted of late to turn Roman Catholic, and nearly did so, but my faith has been much shaken by reading Cardinal Manning's Funeral Sermon for Cardinal Wiseman, over whose death I mourned much. He said that Cardinal Wiseman's last words were: "Let me have all that the Church can do for me!" I seemed to see at once that if the highest ecclesiastic stood thus in need of external rites on his death-bed, the system must be rotten, and I gave up all idea of departing from our Protestant faith.'

From this significant entry, with its revelation of

great thoughts stirring in his soul, I turn to one of a very different kind, yet of no less value.

'*February* 9, 1867: I lost my ring out shooting, with scarcely a hope of ever seeing it again. I offered to give the gamekeeper ten shillings if he found it, and was led to ask God that the ring might be found and be to me *a sure sign of salvation.* From that moment the ring seemed on my finger, and I was not surprised when Sayers brought it to me on Monday evening. He had picked it up in the long grass in cover, a most unlikely place ever to find it. A miracle! Jesus, by Thee alone can we obtain remission of our sins!'

The diary contains a footnote to this entry, written by Hannington some years afterwards. 'This,' he says, 'was written by me· at the most worldly period of my existence.' Yet there it is! These entries prove that, however far from the Kingdom Hannington may then have been, he kept his face turned wistfully and steadfastly towards its gates. The deep religious impulses throbbing in his soul moved him to associate himself with the church; to receive upon his lips the awful mysteries of the Christian sacrament; and, later on, to apply for ordination. But, as he drew nearer to that solemn and searching ceremony, his conscience cried out and his heart failed him.

'How I dread my ordination!' he writes. 'I would willingly draw back; but, when I am tempted to do so, I hear ringing in my ears: "*No man, having put*

*his hand to the plough and looking back is fit for the
Kingdom of God."* What am I to do? What?'

What, indeed? He felt that he was *'not fit for
the Kingdom of God,'* and dare not go on! And
yet, if he turned back, he was only giving fuller
evidence of his unfitness! Here was a dilemma!
He resolved at length to go on, and, in going on,
to seek with full purpose of heart that fitness that
he felt he lacked. 'It is characteristic of the man,'
says his biographer, 'that he should have faced what
he now dreaded with an almost morbid fear. His
conscience would have absolved him on no other
terms. *"No man, having put his hand to the plough,
and looking back, is fit for the Kingdom of God."*
Those words held him fast to his purpose!' So he
made his decision. But the decision did not relieve
his deep spiritual embarrassment, for, whilst he felt
that he dared not look back, he felt that he was
unfit to go on.

'*Not fit for the Kingdom of God!*'
'*Not fit for the Kingdom of God!*'
The words beat themselves into his brain. It was
a terrible situation and he saw no way of escape.

III

The way of escape came by post. It sometimes
does. There are a few choice spirits in God's world
who have mastered the high art of conducting a
religious correspondence. They can write without
gush and without gloom: their letters are neither

sentimental nor sanctimonious. His old comrade
and chum, the Rev. E. C. Dawson, M.A., who
afterwards became his biographer, was, about this
time, greatly concerned on Hannington's behalf.
'I could not tell why,' he says, 'but the burden
seemed to press upon me more heavily day by day.'
At last he resolved to write. He knew Hannington's
scorn of cant, and feared that such a letter would
offend him. 'Still,' he says, 'I reasoned that, if
friendship was to be lost, it should be at least well
lost. So I wrote a simple, unvarnished account of
my own spiritual experience. I tried to explain how
it was that I was not now as formerly. I spoke of
the power of the love of Christ to transform the
life of a man and to draw out all its latent possibili-
ties; and, finally, I urged him, as he loved his own
soul, to make a definite surrender of himself to the
Saviour of the world.' And the result? For the
result we must turn to the diary:

'*July* 15: Dawson, who is now a curate in Surrey,
opened a correspondence with me to-day which I
can only describe as delightful. *It led to my conversion!*'

'I was in bed at the time, reading,' he says, in a
note written years afterwards. 'I sprang out of
bed and leaped about the room rejoicing and praising
God that *Jesus died for me*. From that day to this,
I have lived under the shadow of His wings in the
assurance that I am His and He is mine!'

And, writing to Mr. Dawson, the author of the

letter, he says: 'I have never seen so much light as during the past few days. I know now that *Jesus died for me,* and that He is mine and I am His. I ought daily to be more thankful to you as the instrument by whom I was brought to Christ. Unspeakable joy!'

'It led to my conversion!'
'I know now that Jesus died for me!'
'Unspeakable joy! Unspeakable joy!'

IV

Five years, filled with happy and fruitful ministries, pass away. He is now a proud husband and the father of a little family. All at once, England is stirred to its depths by the news that Lieut. Shergold Smith and Mr. O'Neill have been murdered on the shore of Victoria Nyanza. It affects Hannington like a challenge. He longs to go and fill one of the vacant places. Unable to resist the call, he offers—and is accepted! As the time for his departure approaches, he realises the bitterness of the ordeal that he must face. His people! The congregation is in tears whenever he enters the pulpit. His wife, who had so bravely consented to his application, but who finds it so hard to let him go! His little ones! 'This,' he says, as he records the anguish of farewell, 'this was my most bitter trial—an agony that still cleaves to me—saying good-bye to the little ones. Thank God that all the pain was on one side. Over and over again I thank Him for that! "Come back soon, papa!" they cried. Then the servants, all attached to me. My wife, the bravest of them all!' Over the chapter that tells of such experiences his biographer has inscribed a quotation from Epictetus:

'If some wifeling or childling be granted you, well and good; but, if the Captain call, run to the ship, and leave such possessions behind you, not looking back!'

But, if the work had been an autobiography, and if Hannington himself had chosen the inscription for the heading of that chapter, he would have selected the words that surged through his brain every day and many times a day:

'No man, having put his hand to the plough, and looking back, is fit for the Kingdom of God!'

'No man looking back!' cries the philosopher.

'No man looking back, is fit for the Kingdom of God,' says Hannington's text.

With such words in his heart he fought his way through his valley of weeping and set out for Darkest Africa.

V

But he was driven back, as even the bravest sometimes are. In Africa he was beset by fever after fever. For weeks on end he could not rise from his mattress. His emaciation was terrible to behold. 'Can it be long before I die?' he said one day to Cyril Gordon. 'No,' replied his companion, 'nor can you desire that it should be so!' 'I have a distinct remembrance,' says Mr. Copplestone, another member of the party, 'of one of the few walks which he was able to take with myself. "Copplestone," he said, "I do not think that I can recover from this illness. Let us go that we may choose a place for my grave." So we went, and he selected a spot where he said we were to bury him. He did not expect that he could live long in such a state as that in which he then was.' A day or two later, Mr. Stokes, who had left the party to find a road to the Lake Victoria Nyanza, unexpectedly returned. But let the diary tell its own story:

'*October* 6: Slightly better, but still in very great pain. To our immense surprise, Stokes turned up early this morning. When I heard his voice I exclaimed, "I shall live and not die." It inspired me with new life. I felt that they had returned that I might go with them.'

And so they had! He had to be carried in a hammock, however. In the course of the journey he was often at death's door. Clearly, there was nothing for it but a return to England. Yet, all the way home, he felt that he was beating a retreat.

'*No man, having put his hand to the plough, and looking back, is fit for the Kingdom of God!*' The words haunted him night and day as he paced the deck of the homebound steamer.

'*Forgive the one that turned back!*' It is with

that penitent petition that he closes this chapter of
the diary.

VI

He turned back, but not for long. He had put
his hand to the plough, and he felt that, to show
himself fit for the Kingdom of God, he must faithfully finish the furrow. He had solemnly given
himself to Africa, and he was unwilling to take back
his gift. In 1883, at the age of thirty-six, he found
himself in England, rejoicing in the sweet society
of wife and children and friends. Little by little
his health came back to him; and with its coming,
his old text said its say:

'Not fit for the Kingdom of God!'

*'No man looking back, is fit for the Kingdom of
God!'*

*'No man, having put his hand to the plough, and
looking back, is fit for the Kingdom of God!'*

In Mr. Dawson's great biography, only half a
dozen pages intervene between his arrival in England in June, 1883, and his consecration as Bishop
of Eastern Equatorial Africa, in the June of the
following year. On returning to the dark continent
he is overjoyed at finding his health as robust as it
formerly was precarious. 'I have to praise God,'
he says, in one of his early notes, 'for one of the
most successful journeys, as a journey, that I ever
took. During a tramp of over four hundred miles,
I have enjoyed most excellent health.' He delighted

his friends by completing this preliminary march 'sunburnt and shaggy, but glowing with vigour.' Having thus tested his physical resources, he prepared for his great march to Uganda. The story of that famous and fateful journey need not be retold. It is one of the world's great romances. Everybody knows now that, all unsuspecting, the Bishop went straight to his death. A new king was on the throne: the white men were no longer in favour: the natives were ready to murder the first Englishman they saw. As soon as he drew near to the seat of government, he was seized. 'I felt,' he says in his last journal, 'that I was being dragged away to be murdered; but I sang, "Safe in the Arms of Jesus," and laughed at the very agony of my situation.' Each day, though naked, starving, and racked with excruciating pains, he dots down in his diary the thoughts that comfort him. He can only write two or three words at a time, but he contrives to enter up the journal to the last. 'No news!' he says, in the final entry. 'I was upheld by the thirtieth Psalm, which came with great power. A hyena howled near me last night, smelling a sick man, but I hope it is not to have me yet.' The next day the native warriors, sent by the king, came to kill him. He struggled to his feet, stood erect, and told them that he was glad to die for them and for their people. Seeing them hesitate as to how to end his life, he pointed to his own gun, and, with it, they despatched him. He was only thirty-eight.

To-day a great cathedral marks the spot where he fell. 'Never in my life was I so moved,' says Bishop Tucker, 'as when I preached in that cathedral to a congregation of from four to five thousand people. Many of the communicants bore upon their bodies the scars and disfigurements of their former barbarity.' Clearly he did not die in vain.

'If,' he says, in his last letter, 'if this is the last chapter of my earthly history, then the next will be the first page of the heavenly—no blots and smudges, no incoherence, but sweet converse in the Presence of the Lamb!'

He put his hand to the plough!
He finished his furrow, never looking back!
He was fit for the Kingdom of God!

XVIII

WILLIAM WILBERFORCE'S TEXT

I

THE hand that struck the shackles from the galled limbs of our British slaves was the hand of a hunchback. One of the triumphs of statuary in Westminster Abbey is the seated figure that, whilst faithfully perpetuating the noble face and fine features of Wilberforce, skilfully conceals his frightful physical deformities. From infancy he was an elfish, misshapen little figure. At the Grammar School at Hull, the other boys would lift his tiny, twisted form on to the table and make him go through all his impish tricks. For, though so pitifully stunted and distorted, he was amazingly sprightly, resourceful and clever. A master of mimicry, a born actor, an accomplished singer and a perfect elocutionist, he was as agile, also, as a monkey and as full of mischief. Every day he enlivened his performance by the startling introduction of some fresh antics that convulsed alike his schoolfellows and his teachers. He is the most striking illustration that history can offer of a grotesque and insignificant form glorified by its consecration to a great and noble cause. Recognising the terrible handicap that Nature had imposed upon him, he set himself to counterbalance matters by acquiring a singular graciousness and charm of manner. He succeeded so perfectly that his courtliness and grace became proverbial. It was said of him that, if you saw him in conversation with a man, you would suppose that the man was his brother, or, if with a woman, that he was her lover. He made men forget his strange appearance. When he sprang to his feet to plead the cause of the slave, he seemed like a man inspired, and his disfigurement magically vanished. 'I saw,' says Boswell, in his letter to Mr. Dundas, 'I saw a shrimp mount the table, but, as I listened, he grew and grew until the shrimp became a whale!' When he rose to address the House of Commons, he looked like a dwarf that had jumped out of a fairy-tale; when he resumed his seat, he looked like the giant of the self-same story. His form, as the *Times* said, 'was like the letter S; it resembled a stick that could not be straightened.' Yet his hearers declare that his face, when pleading for the slave, was like the face of an angel. The ugliness of his little frame seemed to disappear; and, under the magic of his passionate eloquence, his form became sublime. When, in 1833, he passed away, such a funeral procession made its way to Westminster Abbey as even London had rarely witnessed. He was borne to his last resting place by the Peers and Commoners of England with the Lord Chancellor at their head. In imperishable

marble it was recorded of him that 'he had removed
from England the guilt of the slave-trade and prepared the way for the abolition of slavery in every
colony in the Empire.' And it is said that, as the
cortège made its sombre way through the crowded
streets, all London was in tears, and one person in
every four was garbed in deepest black.

II

Among Sir James Stephen's masterpieces of bio-
logical analysis, there is nothing finer than his essay
on Wilberforce. But he confesses to a difficulty.
There is, he says, something hidden. You cannot
account for his stupendous influence by pointing to
anything that lies upon the surface. 'What that
hidden life really was,' Sir James observes, 'none
but himself could know, and few indeed could even
plausibly conjecture. But even they who are the
least able to solve the enigma may acknowledge and
feel that there was some secret spring of action on
which his strength was altogether dependent.' Now,
what was that hidden factor? What was the 'secret
spring of action' that explains this strangely-
handicapped yet wonderfully-useful life? Can I
lay my finger on the source of all these beneficent
energies? Can I trace the hidden power that im-
pelled and directed these fruitful and epoch-making
activities? I think I can. Behind all that appears
upon the surface there lies a great experience, a

great thought, *a great text*. I find it at the beginning of his career; I find it again at the close.

As a youth, preparing himself to play some worthy part in life, Wilberforce travels. Thrice he tours Europe, once in the company of William Pitt, then a young fellow of exactly his own age, and twice in the company of Isaac Milner, the brilliant brother of his Hull schoolmaster. It was in the course of one of these tours that the crisis of his inner life overtook him. Milner and he made it a practice to carry with them a few books to read on rainy days. Among these oddly-assorted volumes they slipped into their luggage a copy of Dr. Doddridge's 'Rise and Progress of Religion in the Soul.' It was a dangerous companion for young men who prized their peace of mind; no book of that period had provoked more serious thought. It certainly set Wilberforce thinking; and not all the festivities of his tour nor the laughter of his friends could dispel the feeling that now took sole possession of his mind. One over-powering emotion drove out all others. It haunted him sleeping and waking. 'My sin!' he cried, 'my sin, my sin, my sin!'—it was this thought of his condition that filled him with apprehension and despair.

'The deep guilt and black ingratitude of my past life,' he says, 'forced itself upon me in the strongest colours; and I condemned myself for having wasted my precious time and talents. It was not so much the fear of punishment as a sense of my great sinfulness. Such was the effect which this thought produced that for months I was in a state of the deepest depression from strong conviction of my guilt!'

My deep guilt!
My great sinfulness!
My black ingratitude!

It was then, at the age of twenty-six, that his soul gathered itself up in one great and bitter cry.

'*God be merciful to me a sinner!*' he implored; and, on receiving an assurance that his prayer was heard—as all such prayers must be—he breaks out in a new strain. 'What infinite love,' he says, 'that Christ should die to save *such a sinner!*'

'*My sin! My sin! My sin!*'
'*God be merciful to me a sinner!*'
'*That Christ should die to save such a sinner!*'

This was in 1785. Wilberforce stood then at the dawn of his great day.

For the second scene we must pass over nearly half a century. His career is drawing to its close. The twisted little body is heavily swathed in wrappings and writhes in pain. Hearing of his serious sickness, his Quaker friend, Mr. Joseph Gurney, comes to see him.

'He received me with the warmest marks of affection,' Mr. Gurney says, 'and seemed delighted at the unexpected arrival of an old friend. The illuminated expression of his furrowed countenance, with his clasped and uplifted hands, were indicative of profound devotion and holy joy. He unfolded his experience to me in a highly interesting manner.'

'With regard to myself,' said Mr. Wilberforce, before taking a last farewell of his friend, 'with regard to myself, I have nothing whatever to urge but the poor publican's plea, *"God be merciful to me a sinner!"* '

'These words,' adds Mr. Gurney, 'were expressed with peculiar feeling and emphasis.'

'God be merciful to me a sinner!'—it was the cry of his heart in 1785, as his life lay all before him.

'God be merciful to me a sinner!'—it was still the cry of his heart in 1833, the time when his life lay all behind.

Here, then, is William Wilberforce's text! It will do us good to listen to it as, once and again, it falls from his lips. In outlining the events that led Christiana to forsake the City of Destruction and to follow her husband on pilgrimage, Bunyan tells us that she had a dream, 'And behold, in her dream, she saw as if a broad parchment was opened before her, in which was recorded the sum of her ways; and the times, as she thought, looked very black upon her. Then she cried out aloud in her sleep, *"God be merciful to me a sinner!"* And the little children heard her.' It was well that she cried: it was well that the children heard: it led to their setting out together for the Cross, the Palace Beautiful and the City of Light. It will be well indeed for us if, listening to William Wilberforce as he offers the same agonising petition, we, like Christiana's children, become followers of his faith and sharers of his joy.

III

They are very few, I suppose, who would envy William Wilberforce the wretchedness that darkened his soul at Spa in the course of that third European tour, the wretchedness that led him to cry out for the everlasting mercy. He was then twenty-six; and if any young fellow of twenty-six entertains the slightest doubt as to the desirability of such a mournful experience, I should like to introduce that young fellow first to Robinson Crusoe and then to old William Cottee, of Theydon Bois. We all remember the scene in which Robinson Crusoe, soon after his shipwreck, searched the old chest for tobacco and found—*a Bible!* He began to read. 'It was not long after I set seriously to this work,' he tells us, 'that I found my heart more deeply and sincerely affected with the wickedness of my past life. The impression of my dream revived, and the words, "All these things have not brought thee to repentance," ran seriously in my thoughts. I was earnestly begging of God to give me repentance, when it happened providentially, that very day, that, reading the Scripture, I came to these words, "He is exalted a Prince and a Saviour to give repentance and to give remission." I threw down the book, and, with my heart as well as my hands lifted up to Heaven, in a kind of ecstasy of joy, I cried out aloud, "Jesus, Thou Son of David, Thou exalted Prince and Saviour, give me repentance." This was the first time that I could say, in the true sense of the word, that I prayed in all my life!'

'*Give me repentance!*'—this was Robinson Crusoe's first prayer. But, for William Wilberforce, bemoaning at Spa the list of his transgressions, the prayer is already answered. They may pity him who will: Robinson Crusoe will offer him nothing but congratulations.

So will old William Cottee. The old gentleman was well over ninety, and was bedridden, when, in my college days, I visited him. He has long since passed from his frailty to his felicity. I used occasionally to preach in the village sanctuary, and was more than once the guest of the household that he adorned. No such visit was complete without an invitation to go upstairs and have a talk with grandfather. As a rule, however, those talks with grandfather were a little embarrassing—to a mere student. For a ministerial student moves in an atmosphere in which his theological opinions are treated, to say the least, with respect. He is quite sure of them himself, and he likes other people to exhibit equal confidence. But poor old William Cottee had no respect at all for any theological opinions of mine.

He was a sturdy old hyper-Calvinist, and, to him, the doctrines that I expounded with such assurance were mere milk and water, mostly water. One afternoon I found the old gentleman bewailing the exceeding sinfulness of his evil heart. This seemed to me, viewing the matter from the point of view of a theological student, a very primitive experience for so mature a saint. Perhaps I as good as said so: I forget. I only remember that, in response to my shallow observation, the old gentleman sat straight up in bed—a thing I had never seen him do before—stared at me with eyes so full of reproach that they seemed to pierce my very soul, and slowly recited a verse that I had never before heard and have never since forgotten:

What comfort can a Saviour bring
    To those who never felt their woe?
A sinner is a sacred thing
    The Holy Ghost hath made him so!

Ministers often learn from those they seem to teach; but it rarely happens that a profound and awful and searching truth rushes as startlingly upon a man as this one did that day upon me. It is a hard saying; who can hear it? But the wise will understand. Because of the lesson that he then taught me—to say nothing of the fact that one of his granddaughters has proved for many years the best wife any minister ever had—I have always thought kindly of old William Cottee. I never heard the old man refer to Robinson Crusoe in any way; but I am sure

that he would join the redoubtable islander in con-
gratulating William Wilberforce on the experience
that overtook him in his twenty-sixth year. The
sunlit passages in life are not always the most profit-
able : it is through much tribulation that we enter the
kingdom.

IV

'My sin! My sin! My sin!'
'God be merciful to me a sinner!'
*'What infinite love that Christ should die to save
such a sinner!'*

Wilberforce felt that such infinite love demanded
the fullest requital he could possibly offer. Those
who have been greatly saved must greatly serve. I
like to think of that memorable day on which the
two friends—Wilberforce and Pitt—lay sprawling
on the grass under a grand old oak tree in the beautiful park at Holwood, in Kent. A solid stone seat
now stands beside the tree, bearing an inscription
commemorative of the historic occasion. For it was
then—and there—that Wilberforce solemnly devoted his life to the emancipation of the slaves. He
had introduced the subject with some diffidence;
was delighted at Pitt's evident sympathy; and,
springing to his feet, he declared that he would set
to work at once to abolish the iniquitous traffic. Few
of us realise the immense proportions that the British
slave trade had then assumed. During the eighteenth
century, nearly a million blacks were transported,

with much less consideration than would have been shown to cattle, from Africa to Jamaica alone. From his earliest infancy, the horror of the traffic preyed upon the sensitive mind of William Wilberforce. When quite a boy he wrote to the papers, protesting against 'this odious traffic in human flesh.' Now, a young fellow in the twenties, he made its extinction the purpose of his life. For fifty years he never rested. Through evil report and through good, he tirelessly pursued his ideal. At times the opposition seemed insuperable. But Pitt stood by him; the Quakers and a few others encouraged him to persist; John Wesley, only a few days before his death, wrote begging the reformer never to give up. After twenty years of incessant struggle, it was enacted that the exportation of slaves from Africa should cease; but no relief was offered to those already in bondage. A quarter of a century later, as Wilberforce lay dying, messengers from Westminster entered his room to tell him that at last, at last, the Emancipation Bill had been passed; the slaves were free! 'Thank God!' exclaimed the dying man, 'thank God that I have lived to see this day!' Like Wolfe at Quebec, like Nelson at Trafalgar, like Sir John Franklin in the North-West Passage, he died in the flush of triumph. He had resolved that, as an expression of his gratitude for his own deliverance, he would secure for the slaves their freedom; and he passed away rejoicing that their fetters were all broken and gone.

V

'God be merciful to me a sinner!'—this was his prayer in 1785, as his life lay all before him.

'God be merciful to me a sinner!'—this was his prayer in 1833, as he lay a-dying with his life-work done.

William Wilberforce reminds me of William MacLure. There were many saints in Drumtochty, but there was no greater saint than old Dr. MacLure. Rich and poor, young and old; the good doctor on his white pony had fought his way through the dark nights and the deep snowdrifts of the glen to help and heal them all. And now he is dying himself! Drumsheugh sits beside the bed. The doctor asks him to read a bit. Drumsheugh puts on his spectacles.

'Ma mither,' he says, 'aye wanted this read tae her when she was sairly sick,' and he begins to read 'In My Father's house are many mansions . . . .' But the doctor stops him.

'It's a bonnie word,' he says, 'but it's no for the likes o' me!' And he makes him read the parable of the Pharisee and the Publican till he comes to the words, *'God be merciful to me a sinner!'*

'That micht hae been written for me, Drumsheugh, or any ither auld sinner that has feenished his life, an' hes naething tae say for himself.'

Exactly so spake William Wilberforce. Mr.

Gurney quoted many great and comfortable Scriptures, but the dying man shook his head.

'With regard to myself,' he said, 'I have nothing whatever to urge but the poor publican's plea, *"God be merciful to me a sinner!"'*

In what better company than in the company of William MacLure and William Wilberforce can we enter the kingdom of God?

XIX

JOHN WESLEY'S TEXT

I

JOHN WESLEY made history wholesale. 'You cannot cut him out of our national life,' Mr. Augustine Birrell declares. If you could, the gap would be as painful as though you had overthrown the Nelson column in Trafalgar Square or gashed Mount Everest out of the Himalaya Ranges. Lecky, who is a pastmaster in the art of analysing great movements and in tracing the psychological influences from which they sprang, says that the conversion of John Wesley formed one of the grand epochs of English history. His conversion, mark you! Lecky goes on to say that the religious revolution begun in England by the preaching of the Wesleys is of greater historic importance than all the splendid victories by land and sea won under Pitt. The momentous event to which the historian points, be it noted, is not Wesley's birth, but his re-birth. It is his conversion that counts. In order that I may scrutinise once more the record of that tremendous event in our national annals, I turn afresh to Wesley's journal. It was on May 24, 1738. Wesley was engaged in those days in a persistent and passionate quest.

He had crossed the Atlantic as a missionary only to discover the waywardness and wickedness of his own evil heart. 'What have I learned?' he asks himself when he finds himself once more on English soil. 'What have I learned? Why, I have learned what I least of all suspected, that I, who went to America to convert the Indians, was never myself converted to God!' One day, early in 1738, he is chatting with three of his friends when all at once they begin to speak of their faith, the faith that leads to pardon, the faith that links a man with God, the faith that brings joy and peace through believing. Wesley feels that he would give the last drop of his blood to secure for himself such an unspeakable treasure. Could such a faith be his? he asks his companions. 'They replied with one mouth that this faith was the gift, the free gift of God, and that He would surely bestow it upon every soul who earnestly and perseveringly sought it.' Wesley made up his mind that, this being so, it should be his. 'I resolved to seek it unto the end,' he says. 'I continued to seek it,' he writes again, 'until May 24, 1738.' And, on May 24, 1738, he found it! That Wednesday morning, before he went out, he opened his Bible haphazard, and a text leapt out at him. *Thou art not very far from the kingdom of God!* It strangely reassured him.

'The kingdom of God!'
'Far from the kingdom of God!'
'Not very far from the kingdom of God!'

How far? He was so near that, that very evening, he entered it! *'In the evening,'* he says, in the entry that has become one of the monuments of English literature, *'in the evening I went very unwillingly to a society in Aldersgate Street, where one was reading Luther's preface to the Epistle to the Romans. About a quarter before nine, while he was describing the change which God works in the heart through faith in Christ, I felt my heart strangely warmed. I felt I did trust in Christ, Christ alone, for salvation: and an assurance was given me that He had taken away my sins, even mine, and saved me from the laws of sin and death.'*

Here is a sailor! He finds himself far, far from port, with no chart, no compass, no hope of ever reaching his desired haven! Later on, he shades his eyes with his hand and actually sees the bluff headlands that mark the entrance to the harbor: he is not very far from the city of his desire! And, later still, the bar crossed and the channel found, he finds himself lying at anchor in the bay.

So it was with John Wesley. When he returned from Georgia, he was far, very far from the kingdom of God. When he opened his Bible that Wednesday morning, he was not very far from the kingdom of God. And that same evening, at Aldersgate Street, he passed through the gates into the light and liberty of the kingdom.

So far from the kingdom!
Not far from the kingdom!

The kingdom! The kingdom! The kingdom of God!

II

It is a beautiful thing to have been brought near to the kingdom of God. Many influences combined to bring John Wesley near. To begin with, he had a mother; one of the most amazing mothers that even England—that land of noble mothers—has produced. Susanna Wesley was a marvel of nature and a miracle of grace. To begin with, she was the twenty-fifth child of her father; and, to go on with, she had nineteen children of her own! And she found time for each of them. In one of her letters, she tells how deeply impressed she was on reading the story of the evangelistic efforts of the Danish missionaries in India. 'It came into my mind,' she says, 'that I might do more than I do. I resolved to begin with my own children. I take such proportion of time as I can best spare to discourse every night with each child by itself.' Later on, people began to marvel at her remarkable influence over her children. 'There is no mystery about the matter,' she writes again, 'I just took Molly alone with me into my own room every Monday night, Hetty every Tuesday night, Nancy every Wednesday night, Jacky every Thursday night, and so on, all through the week; that was all!' Yes, that was all; but see how it turned out! 'I cannot remember,' says John Wesley, 'I cannot remember ever having kept back a doubt from my mother; she was the one heart to whom I went in absolute confidence, from my babyhood until the day of her death.' Such an influence could only tend to bring him *near to the kingdom of God*.

Then there was the fire! John never forgot that terrible night. He was only six. He woke up to find the old rectory ablaze from the ground to the roof. By some extraordinary oversight, he had been forgotten when everybody else was dragged from the burning building. In the nick of time, just before the roof fell in with a crash, a neighbour, by climbing on another man's shoulders, contrived to rescue the terrified child at the window. To the last day of his life Wesley preserved a crude picture of the scene. And underneath it was written, 'Is not this a brand plucked from the burning?' It affected him as a somewhat similar escape affected Clive. 'Surely God intends to do some great thing by me that He has so miraculously preserved me!' exclaimed the man who afterwards added India to the British Empire. When a young fellow of eighteen, Richard Baxter was thrown by a restive horse under the wheel of a heavy waggon. Quite unaccountably, the horse instantly stopped. 'My life was miraculously saved,' he wrote, 'and I then and there resolved that it should be spent in the service of others.' Dr. Guthrie regarded as one of the potent spiritual influences of his life his marvellous deliverance from being dashed to pieces over

a precipice at Arbroath. In his 'Grace Abounding,'
Bunyan tells how he was affected by the circumstance that the man who took his place at the siege
of Leicester was shot through the head whilst on
sentry-duty and killed instantly. Such experiences
tend to bring men within sight of the kingdom of
God. Wesley never forgot the fire.

III

*It is a great thing to recognise that, though near
to the kingdom, one is still outside.*

Sir James Simpson, the discoverer of chloroform,
used to say that the greatest discovery that he ever
made was the discovery that he was a sinner and that
Jesus Christ was just the Saviour he needed. John
Wesley could have said the same. But, whereas
Sir James Simpson was able to point to the exact
date on which the sense of his need broke upon him,
John Wesley is not so explicit. He tells us that it
was in Georgia that he discovered that he, the would-
be converter of Indians, was himself unconverted.
And yet, before he left England, he wrote to a
friend that his chief motive in going abroad was the
salvation of his own soul. As soon as he arrived
on the other side of the Atlantic, he made the acquaintance of August Spangenberg, a Moravian
pastor. A conversation took place which Wesley
records in his journal as having deeply impressed
him.

'My brother,' said the devout and simple-minded

man whose counsel he had sought, 'I must ask you one or two questions: Do you know Jesus Christ?'

'I know,' replied Wesley, after an awkward pause, 'I know that he is the Saviour of the world.'

'True,' answered the Moravian, 'but do you know that He has saved *you?*'

'I hope He has died to save me,' Wesley responded.

The Moravian was evidently dissatisfied with these vague replies, but he asked one more question.

'Do you know yourself!'

'I said that I did,' Wesley tells us in his journal, 'but I fear they were vain words!'

He saw others happy, fearless in the presence of death, rejoicing in a faith that seemed to transfigure their lives. What was it that was *theirs* and yet not *his?* 'Are they read in philosophy?' he asks. 'So was I. In ancient or modern tongues? So was I also. Are they versed in the science of divinity? I, too, have studied it many years. Can they talk fluently upon spiritual things? I could do the same. Are they plenteous in alms? Behold, I give all my goods to feed the poor! I have laboured more abundantly than they all. Are they willing to suffer for their brethren? I have thrown up my friends, reputation, ease, country; I have put my life in my hand, wandering into strange lands; I have given my body to be devoured by the deep, parched up with heat, consumed by toil and weariness. But does all this make me acceptable to God! Does all this make me a Christian? By no means! I have sinned and come short of the glory of God. I am alienated from the life of God. I am a child of wrath. I have no hope.' It is a great thing, I say, for a man who has been brought within sight of the kingdom to recognise frankly that he is, nevertheless, still outside it.

IV

It is a fine thing for a man who feels that he is outside the kingdom to enter into it.

In his 'Cheapside to Arcady,' Mr. Arthur Scammell describes the pathetic figure of an old man he often saw in a London slum. 'He had crept forth from some poor house hard by, and, propped up by a crutch, was sitting on the edge of a low wall in the unclean, sunless alley, whilst, only a few yards further on, was the pleasant open park, with sunshine, trees and flowers, the river and fresh air, and, withal, a more comfortable seat: but the poor old man never even looked that way. I have often seen him since, always in the same place, and felt that I should like to ask him why he sits there in darkness, breathing foul air, when the blessed sunshine is waiting for him only ten yards off.'

So near to the sunshine!

So near to the kingdom!

Unlike Mr. Scammell's old man, John Wesley made the great transition from shadow to sunshine, from squalor to song.

'Dost thou believe,' asked Staupitz, the wise old monk, 'dost thou believe in the forgiveness of sins?'

'I believe,' replied Luther, reciting a clause from his familiar credo, 'I believe in the forgiveness of sins!'

'Ah,' exclaimed the elder monk, 'but you must not only believe in the forgiveness of David's sins and Peter's sins, for this even the devils believe. It is God's command that we believe *our own sins* are forgiven us!'

'From that moment,' says D'Aubigne, 'light sprung up in the heart of the young monk at Erfurt.'

'I believed,' says Luther, 'that *my sins, even mine, were forgiven me!*'

'I did trust in Christ, Christ alone, for salvation,' says Wesley, in his historic record, 'and an assurance was given me that He had taken away *my sins, even mine!*'

The analogy is suggested by the circumstance that it was Luther's commentary that was being read aloud at Aldersgate Street that night.

'*My sins, even mine!*' says Luther.

'*My sins, even mine!*' says Wesley.

Forty-five years afterwards Mr. Wesley was taken very ill at Bristol and expected to die. Calling Mr. Badford to his bedside, he observed: 'I have been reflecting on my past life. I have been wandering up and down, these many years, endeavouring, in my poor way, to do a little good to my fellow-creatures; and now it is probable that there is but

a step between me and death; and what have I to
trust to for salvation? I can see nothing which I
have done or suffered that will bear looking at. I
have no other plea than this:

> "I the chief of sinners am,
> But Jesus died for me."'

Eight years later—fifty-three years after the great
change at Aldersgate Street—he was actually dying.
As his friends surrounded his bedside, he told them
that he had no more to say. 'I said at Bristol,' he
murmured, 'that

> "I the chief of sinners am,
> But Jesus died for me."'

'Is that,' one asked, 'the present language of your
heart, and do you feel now as you did then?' 'I do,'
replied the dying veteran.

This, then, was the burden of Wesley's tremendous ministry for more than fifty-three years.
It was the confidence of his life and the comfort of
his death. It was his first thought every morning
and his last every night. It was the song of his
soul, the breath of his nostrils, and the light of his
eyes. This was the gospel that transfigured his own
experience; and this was the gospel by which he
changed the face of England 'John Wesley,' says
Mr. Birrell, 'paid more turnpikes than any man who
ever bestrode a beast. Eight thousand miles was
his annual record for many a long year, during each
of which he seldom preached less frequently than a

thousand times. No man ever lived nearer the centre than John Wesley, neither Clive, nor Pitt, nor Johnson. No single figure influenced so many minds; no single voice touched so many hearts. No other man did such a life's work for England.' 'The eighteenth century,' says President Wilson, 'cried out for deliverance and light; and God prepared John Wesley to show the world the might and the blessing of His salvation.'

V

The pity of it is that John Wesley was thirty-five when he entered the kingdom. The zest and vigour of his early manhood had passed. He was late in finding mercy. Thirty-five! Before they reached that age, men like Murray McCheyne, Henry Martyn, and David Brainerd had finished their life-work and fallen into honoured graves. Why was Wesley's great day so long in coming? He always felt that the fault was not altogether his own. He groped in the dark for many years and nobody helped him—not even his ministers. William Law was one of those ministers, and Wesley afterwards wrote him on the subject. 'How will you answer to our common Lord,' he asks, 'that you, sir, never led me into the light? Why did I scarcely ever hear you name *the name of Christ?* Why did you never urge me to *faith in his blood?* Is not Christ the First and the Last? If you say that you thought I had faith already, verily, you know nothing of me. I beseech you, sir, by the mercies of God, to consider whether the true reason of your never pressing this salvation upon me was not this—*that you never had it yourself!'*

Here is a letter for a man like Wesley to write to a man like Law! Many a minister has since read that letter on his knees and has prayed that he may never deserve to receive so terrible a reprimand.

XX

WILLIAM KNIBB'S TEXT

I

COULD anything be more perfectly beautiful, more wonderfully fair? Far as the eye can reach in every direction, the eye is charmed and captivated by the loveliness of the landscape. As we pace the deck of the steamer as she rides at anchor in the bay, we we turn from one prospect to another, uncertain as to which of them all is the most delightful. In the background the Blue Mountains stand out in sturdy and rugged grandeur against the deep blue sky. Even at this distance, we get hints of the glorious forests that clothe those graceful slopes, and of the thickly-wooded valleys that divide range from range. What a playground for the countless troops of monkeys! What a paradise for the flocks of gorgeously-coloured birds! Their gay plumage flashes like flames of fire amidst this riot of gigantic forestry! Nearer to the coast are the vast plains which, built up in the course of ages by tiny coral insects, now wave with their flourishing plantations and abounding fruitage. For the island is as fertile as it is fair, as rich as it is radiant! Coffee and sugar and arrowroot; orange and lemon and grape; cinnamon, banana and pineapple; this oval beauty spot in sunbathed tropical seas is a congenial garden for them all! Even the ocean that caresses the island seems to feel that it must assume a beauty in keeping with the loveliness of the land its waters lave. The masses of brilliant coral immediately beneath the surface impart to the shining waters a sheen of sapphire tints such as the sea but rarely boasts. 'I have spent many years,' says a modern traveller, 'in voyaging from shore to shore; but I know of no spot under heaven where the land is so luxuriously beautiful and the ocean so extravagantly blue.' This, then, is Jamaica!

II

Could anything be more abominable, more repulsively hideous? Life in this scene of enchantment was the life, not of paradise, but of perdition. From these fruitful plains and flowery valleys there rose to heaven, not a song of praise, but a scream of intolerable anguish. For Jamaica was the abode of slavery. All day long the men must work, and all day long the women must weep. But the men will derive no satisfaction from their labour and the women will find no comfort in their tears. They are not their own, these people; far less are they each other's. There is no such thing as marriage among these ebony-skinned, thick-lipped, woolly-haired creatures: and any unions that they form among themselves are subject to the exigencies of future sales. These little children in which the missionaries interest themselves, children with roguish eyes and laughing faces, have been bred for the market, and they will be sold as soon as their limbs are set. Young men and maidens are pretty much the same all the world over; you may see a good deal of furtive lovemaking of an evening among the plantations. But in each lover's heart there is a dagger that Cupid never shot. For, as the stalwart youth sees his dusky sweetheart growing more shapely and more charming, he trembles lest her beauty should catch the eye of her overseer and result in her being sold to a life that is worse than a thousand deaths. The best that he can hope for is that he and she may be permitted to live together for a few years in some little hut among the bushes to produce children for sale at the monthly market. And if any slave dares to lift up his hand, or even his voice, in rebellion or resentment, there are the treadmill and the lash and the knife. The only thing that stands between the black man and a cruel death is his market value on the plantation or at the auction block. Like the asp that Cleopatra concealed among the lilies, this hideous evil cried to heaven from among the beauteous fields and forests of Jamaica. Did heaven hear such piercing cries? And, even if heaven heard, how could heaven help? We shall see! But in order to see we must re-cross the Atlantic!

III

And here, in a narrow street in Bristol, is a printer's shop. The name over the door, comparatively freshly painted, is the name of J. G Fuller. In the printing-room behind the shop are a couple of apprentice boys. They are brothers—Thomas and William Knibb. Mr. Fuller is the son of the Rev. Andrew Fuller of Kettering, one of the founders of the modern missionary movement. He has only recently come to Bristol, hence the newly-painted name; and he brought the two Knibbs, Kettering boys, with him. Mr. Fuller, with the impress of his father's noble character strongly upon him, at once associates himself with the Broadmead Church and Sunday School. After awhile the two apprentices, with the impress of their employer's character strongly upon them, associate themselves with the same church and take classes in the same Sunday School. It is a fine thing when a man's piety is of such an order that the youths in his workroom say among themselves: 'His religion shall be my religion and his God my God!' In due time Mr. Fuller became superintendent of the Sunday School, and made it his practice to deliver a short address before closing the school. It was one of those addresses that made history. I have heard of a man aiming at a pigeon and killing a crow, but I know of no instance in which that remarkable feat was performed on such a splendid scale as in the conversion of William Knibb. One Sunday afternoon, before dismissing the children, Mr. Fuller spoke for a few moments from the text: *'Wilt Thou not from this time cry unto me, My Father, Thou art the guide of my youth?'* Mr. Fuller aimed at the scholars, but his words smote the conscience and won the heart of a teacher, and that teacher one of his own apprentices! 'It was a most earnest and affectionate address,' wrote William Knibb, shortly afterwards, 'and, under the divine blessing, it made a deep and, I trust, a lasting impression on my mind, and I hope that I was enabled to cast myself at the foot of the Cross as a perishing sinner, pleading for mercy for the sake of Jesus Christ and for His sake alone!' A day or two later the youth sought an interview with his employer. 'I felt ashamed,' said Knibb, in the course of this conversation with Mr. Fuller, 'I felt ashamed, being a teacher, that the address should be as suitable to me as to the children. I felt conscious that I had wandered as far from God as ever they had, and that I needed a forgiving Father and a constant guide as much as they did. I was overwhelmed. I felt such a mixture of shame and grief, of hope and love, as I had never felt before and cannot now describe. I could not join in the closing hymn. I went to my room above and yielded to my feelings. I wept bitterly and prayed as I had never prayed before. I turned the text itself into a prayer. *"My Father,"* I cried to God, *"wilt not Thou from this time be the guide of my youth?"* The Lord heard my prayer and enabled me to give Him my heart; and now it is my earnest desire to yield myself to His guidance as long as I live!'

'*I needed a forgiving Father!*'

'*I needed a constant Guide!*'

'*My Father, wilt not Thou be the guide of my youth?*'

'The Lord heard my prayer!' the apprentice says exultingly, as he looks gratefully into his employer's face. And when the Lord heard that prayer, He heard the bitter cry of the island whose fair shores we just now visited; for the salvation of William Knibb was the deliverance of the slaves across the seas.

IV

And yet it was not *William* Knibb, but *Thomas,* who was most concerned about the lands that lay in darkness. In setting up some copy that had come into the printing-room, the elder of the two apprentices had been startled by the crying needs of the heathen world. He longed to be a missionary. When, one day, somebody referred to the successes being achieved by native preachers, Thomas burst into tears. His younger brother asked him why he wept. 'I am greatly afraid,' Thomas replied, 'that, since the native preachers are so successful, no more white missionaries will be needed; and I shall have no part in the evangelisation of the world!' His fears, however, were groundless. He became a missionary; was designated for Jamaica; arrived there in January, 1823; and died of malaria just three months later. It was a dark day for the younger brother when the heavy tidings reached England. But he met the crisis, his biographer tells us, with characteristic firmness and promptitude. When the news of his brother's death was communicated to him by Mr. Fuller, his feelings were strongly excited and he wept bitterly. But, as soon as the first gush of emotion had subsided, he rose from the table and said: 'Then, if the society will accept me, I'll go and take his place!'

A forgiving Father!

A constant Guide!

'My Father, wilt not Thou be the guide of my youth?'

In the cry of an enslaved people, fortified and intensified by a cry from his brother's grave, William Knibb recognised the leading of the Kindly Light. The 'Guide of his Youth' was pointing the way, and he bravely followed the gleam.

V

'My Father,' he cried, on that never-to-be-forgotten Sunday afternoon, *'will not Thou be the guide of my youth?'* And not once, through all the eventful years that followed, did that clear guidance fail him! He went out to Jamaica to preach the gospel; but he soon came to feel—as Livingstone felt on the

other side of the Atlantic a few years afterwards—
that the work of evangelisation and the work of
emancipation are inseparable. Christianity could
make no terms with slavery. Little by little he was
led, by the Invisible Guide whose beckoning hand he
had pledged himself to follow, into a work that he
had never for a moment anticipated. The sights that
he witnessed sickened him; they became the ceaseless torture of his soul. He felt that no sacrifice
would be too great if only he could strike the
shackles from the limbs of the slaves. And he made
terrific sacrifices! The guidance that he had so
passionately sought rarely led him in green pastures
or beside still waters. It led him, rather, into terrible privations, relentless persecution and desolating
bereavements. In that fever-laden climate he, one
by one, buried his children almost as soon as they
were born. One, the boy whom he named after himself, was spared to see his twelfth birthday, but the
others were lowered as babes into his brother's grave.
From one of these heart-rending burials after another he turned sadly away, the father-soul within
him longing for life in a land in which his little ones
could live. But the reformer-soul within him determined never to leave the island till all the slaves
were free. On more than one occasion he was
charged with rebellion, handcuffed, and dragged
about the island, his persecutors heaping upon him
every form of indignity that would be calculated to
degrade him in the eyes of the slaves. The churches

that he had erected at such cost, and in which he
had taken such pride, were burned down by the
slave-owners before his very eyes. He was spared
no humiliation that could tend to his embarrassment
and discomfiture. He visited England in order that
he might stir his fellow-countrymen to righteous indignation. The whole country was moved by the
passion and the pathos of those tremendous appeals.
'If I fail in arousing the sympathy of England,' he
cried, 'I will go back to Jamaica and call upon Him
who hath made of one blood all nations upon the
earth. And if I die without beholding the emancipation of my brethren and sisters in Christ, then,
if prayer is permitted in Heaven, I will fall at the
feet of the Eternal, crying: "Lord, open the eyes
of Christians in England to see the evil of slavery
and to banish it from the earth!"' But the people
heard; and the Parliament heard; and the prayer
of his passionate heart was granted him.

VI

'Wilt not Thou be the Guide of my youth?' he
cried.

And the Guide led to the goal! As a result of
Mr. Knibb's tireless activities, the slaves were freed!
Their emancipation came into force at midnight on
July 31, 1838. And what is this? As the historic
hour draws near, the exultant slaves gather in their
thousands at the church. During the evening,
hymns are sung, the excited blacks joining in the

praise with a zest that even they have never shown before. As the night deepens the emotion becomes more intense. As the hand of the clock approaches the midnight hour, Mr. Knibb, standing in the pulpit, shouts, 'The Monster is dying!' As the clock begins to strike he cries again: 'The Monster is dying!' And when the hour has fully struck he proclaims: 'The Monster is dead!' The scene is indescribable. 'Never,' wrote Knibb, 'was heard such a sound. The winds of freedom appeared to have been let loose. The very building shook at the strange, yet sacred, joy. Oh, had my boy, my lovely, freedom-loving boy, been there! Alas, he is sleeping undisturbed in the churchyard, nor can the sweet sounds he so much loved awake him from his rest!' In passionate longing to have at least one of his children associated with that glad historic event, Mr. Knibb slips across to his home, draws his twelve-months' old baby from his cot, and, midnight though it is, returns with the child in his arms, and holds him proudly up before the shouting, clapping, singing multitude. In the early grey of the morning, a most remarkable burial takes place in the churchyard. One might almost say, in the words of Mrs. Alexander:

> That was the grandest funeral
> That ever passed on earth.

Many of the slaves are skilled cabinet-makers. They have prepared a most exquisitely-carved and polished coffin, and have dug a deep, deep grave. Into the coffin they throw the slave-chain, a slave-whip, a slave-hat, and an iron collar—all the insignia of their degradation. The great crowd of grateful freemen gathers round the open grave and a solemn funeral service is held. At the proper moment, the coffin is lowered into the yawning grave, the multitude singing exultingly:

> 'Now, Slavery, we lay thy vile form in the dust,
>   And, buried for ever, there let it remain:
> And rotted, and covered with infamy's rust,
>   Be every man-whip and fetter and chain.'

The land rings with doxologies. The beauteous island is delivered from its hideous curse! The Guide has led to the goal! The chains are shattered! The slaves are free!

VII

Among the people whom he loved so well, the people whom he had emancipated and evangelised, Knibb died a few years later. He was only forty-two when he passed away. 'I am not afraid to die,' he said, 'the blood of Jesus Christ cleanseth from all sin, both of omission and commission; that blood is my only trust!' And, just as the gentle spirit was about to take its flight, he reached out his hand to Mrs. Knibb and murmured: 'Mary, it is all right: all is well!'

'My Father,' he cried, at the dawn of his career,

'My Father, will not Thou be the Guide of my youth?'

'It is all right: all is well!' he murmured in the last moments of his life.

The Guide had led to the goal! Under sure, safe, skilful pilotage, the ship had made a good voyage and had come straight to port! William Knibb had cast his anchor within the veil! 'It is all right: all is well!' Such is the final gladness of all who follow faithfully the Kindly Light!

XXI

JOHN NEWTON'S TEXT

I

JOHN NEWTON was plagued with a terribly treacherous memory. In his youth it had betrayed and nearly ruined him; how could he ever trust it again? 'You must know,' said Greatheart to Christiana's boys, 'you must know that Forgetful Green is the most dangerous place in all these parts.' John Newton understood, better than any man who ever lived, exactly what Greatheart meant. Poor John Newton nearly lost his soul on Forgetful Green. His autobiography is filled with the sad, sad story of his forgettings. 'I forgot,' he says again and again and again, 'I forgot . . .! I soon forgot . . .! This, too, I totally forgot!' The words occur repeatedly. And so it came to pass that when, after many wild and dissolute years, he left the sea and entered the Christian ministry, he printed a certain text in bold letters, and fastened it right across the wall over his study mantelpiece:

> THOU SHALT REMEMBER THAT THOU WAST
> A BONDMAN IN THE LAND OF EGYPT, AND
> THE LORD THY GOD REDEEMED THEE.

A photograph of that mantelpiece lies before me as I write. There, clearly enough, hangs John Newton's text! In sight of it he prepared every sermon. In this respect John Newton resembled Thomas Goodwin. 'When,' says that sturdy Puritan, in a letter to his son, 'when I was threatening to become cold in my ministry, and when I felt Sabbath morning coming and my heart not filled with amazement at the grace of God, or when I was making ready to dispense the Lord's Supper, do you know what I used to do? I used to take a turn up and down among the sins of my past life, and I always came down again with a broken and contrite heart, ready to preach, as it was preached in the beginning, the forgiveness of sins.' 'I do not think,' he says again, 'I ever went up the pulpit stair that I did not stop for a moment at the foot of it and take a turn up and down among the sins of my past years. I do not think that I ever planned a sermon that I did not take a turn round my study-table and look back at the sins of my youth and of all my life down to the present; and many a Sabbath morning, when my soul had been cold and dry for the lack of prayer during the week, a turn up and down in my past life before I went into the pulpit always broke my hard heart and made me close with the gospel for my own soul before I began to preach.' Like this great predecessor of his, Newton felt that, in his pulpit preparation, he must keep his black, black past ever vividly before his eyes.

*'I forgot . . .! I soon forgot . . .! This, too,
I totally forgot!'*

'Thou shalt remember, remember, remember!'

*'Thou shalt remember that thou wast a bondman
in the land of Egypt, and that the Lord thy God
redeemed thee!'*

II

'A bondman!'

*'Thou shalt remember that thou wast a bond-
man!'*

The words were literally true! For some time
Newton was a slavetrader; but, worse still, for some
time he was a slave! Newton's conversion deserves
to be treasured among the priceless archives of the
Christian church because of the amazing transformation it effected. It seems incredible that an
Englishman could fall as low as he did. As Professor Goldwin Smith says, he was a brand plucked
from the very heart of the burning! Losing his
mother—the one clear guiding-star of his early life
—when he was seven, he went to sea when he was
eleven. 'I went to Africa,' he tells us, 'that I might
be free to sin to my heart's content.' During the
next few years his soul was seared by the most
revolting and barbarous of all human experiences.
He endured the extreme barbarities of a life before
the mast; he fell into the pitiless clutches of the
pressgang; as a deserter from the navy he was
flogged until the blood streamed down his back;

and he became involved in the unspeakable atrocities
of the African slave trade. And then, going from
bad to worse, he actually became a slave himself!
The slave of a slave! He was sold to a negress
who, glorying in her power over him, made him
depend for his food on the crusts that she tossed
under her table! He could sound no lower depth
of abject degradation. In the after-years, he could
never recall this phase of his experience without a
shudder. As he says in the epitaph that he composed for himself, he was 'the slave of slaves.'

'*A bondman!*'

'*A slave of slaves! A bondman of bondmen!*'

'*Thou shalt remember that thou wast a bond-
man!*'

How could he ever forget?

III

How, I say, could he ever forget? And yet he
had forgotten other things scarcely less notable.

As a boy, he was thrown from a horse and nearly
killed. Looking death in the face in this abrupt and
untimely way, a deep impression was made. 'But,'
he says, '*I soon forgot!*'

Some years later, he made an appointment with
some companions to visit a man-of-war. They were
to meet at the waterside at a certain time and row
out to the battleship. But the unexpected happened.
Newton was detained; his companions left without

him; the boat was upset and they were drowned. 'I went to the funeral,' Newton says, 'and was exceedingly affected. *But this, also, I soon forgot!*'

Then came a remarkable dream. Really, he was lying in his hammock in the forecastle of a ship homeward bound from Italy. But, in his fancy, he was back at Venice. It was midnight; the ship, he thought, was riding at anchor; and it was his watch on deck. As, beneath a clear Italian sky, he paced to and fro across the silent vessel, a stranger suddenly approached him. This mysterious visitant gave him a beautiful ring. 'As long as you keep it,' he said, 'you will be happy and successful; but, if you lose it, you will know nothing but trouble and misery.' The stranger vanished. Shortly after, a second stranger appeared on deck. The newcomer pointed to the ring. 'Throw it away!' he cried, 'throw it away!' Newton was horrified at the proposal; but he listened to the arguments of the stranger and at length consented. Going to the side of the ship, he flung the ring into the sea. Instantly the land seemed ablaze with a range of volcanoes in fierce eruption, and he understood that all those terrible flames had been lit for his destruction. The second stranger vanished; and, shortly after, the first returned. Newton fell at his feet and confessed everything. The stranger entered the water and regained the ring. 'Give it me!' Newton cried, in passionate entreaty, 'give it me!' 'No,' replied the stranger, 'you have shown that you are unable to keep it! I will preserve it for you, and, whenever you need it, will produce it on your behalf.' 'This dream,' says Newton, 'made a very great impression; but the impression soon wore off, and, in a little time, *I totally forgot it!*

'*I forgot!*'

'*This, too, I soon forgot!*'

'*In a little time, I totally forgot it!*'

So treacherous a thing was Newton's memory! Is it any wonder that he suspected it, distrusted it, feared it? Is it any wonder that, right across his study wall, he wrote that text?

'*Thou shalt remember!*'

'*Thou shalt remember that thou wast a bond-man!*'

'*Thou shalt remember that thou wast a bond-man, and that the Lord thy God redeemed thee!*'

IV

'*Thou shalt remember that thou wast a bond-man!*'

'*Thou shalt remember that the Lord thy God redeemed thee!*'

But how? Was the work of grace in John Newton's soul a sudden or a gradual one? It is difficult to say. It is always difficult to say. The birth of the body is a very sudden and yet a very gradual affair: so also is the birth of the soul. To say that John Newton was *suddenly* converted would be to

ignore those gentle and gracious influences by which
two good women—his mother and his sweetheart—
led him steadily heavenwards. 'I was born,' Newton himself tells us, ' in a home of godliness, and
dedicated to God in my infancy. I was my mother's
only child, and almost her whole employment was
the care of my education.' Every day of her life
she prayed with him as well as for him, and every
day she sought to store his mind with those majestic
and gracious words that, once memorised, can never
be altogether shaken from the mind. It was the
grief of her deathbed that she was leaving her boy,
a little fellow of seven, at the mercy of a rough
world; but she had sown the seed faithfully, and
she hoped for a golden harvest.

Some years later, John Newton fell in love with
Mary Catlett. She was only thirteen—the age of
Shakespeare's Juliet. But his passion was no passing fancy. 'His affection for her,' says Professor
Goldwin Smith, 'was as constant as it was romantic;
his father frowned on the engagement, and he became estranged from home; but through all his
wanderings and sufferings he never ceased to think
of her; and after seven years she became his wife.'
The Bishop of Durham, in a centennial sermon, declares that Newton's pure and passionate devotion
to this simple and sensible young girl was 'the one
merciful anchor that saved him from final self-
abandonment.' Say that Newton's conversion was
sudden, therefore, and you do a grave injustice to

the memory of two women whose fragrant influence should never be forgotten.

And yet it *was* sudden; so sudden that Newton could tell the exact date and name the exact place! It took place on the tenth of March, 1748, on board a ship that was threatening to founder in the grip of a storm. *'That tenth of March,'* says Newton, *'is a day much to be remembered by me; and I have never suffered it to pass unnoticed since the year 1748. For on that day—March 10, 1748—the Lord came from on high and delivered me out of deep waters.'* The storm was terrific: when the ship went plunging down into the trough of the seas few on board expected her to come up again. The hold was rapidly filling with water. As Newton hurried to his place at the pumps he said to the captain, 'If this will not do, the Lord have mercy upon us!' His own words startled him.

'Mercy!' he said to himself, in astonishment, 'mercy! *mercy!* What mercy can there be for me? This was the first desire I had breathed for mercy for many years! About six in the evening the hold was free from water, and then came a gleam of hope. I thought I saw the hand of God displayed in our favour. I began to pray. I could not utter the prayer of faith. I could not draw near to a reconciled God and call Him Father. My prayer for mercy was like the cry of the ravens, which yet the Lord Jesus does not disdain to hear.'

'In the gospel,' says Newton, in concluding the

story of his conversion, 'in the gospel I saw at least
a peradventure of hope; but on every other side I
was surrounded with black, unfathomable despair.'
On that 'peradventure of hope' Newton staked
everything.   On the tenth of   March, 1748, he
sought mercy—and found it! He was then twenty-
three.

V

Years afterwards, when he entered the Christian
ministry, John Newton began making history. He
made it well. His hand is on the nation still. He
changed the face of England. He began with the
church. In his 'History of the Church of England,'
Wakeman gives us a sordid and terrible picture of
the church as Newton found it. The church was in
the grip of the political bishop, the fox-hunting
parson, and an utterly worldly and materialistic
laity. Spiritual leadership was unknown. John
Newton and a few kindred spirits, 'the first generation of the clergy called "evangelical," ' became—to
use Sir James Stephen's famous phrase—'the second
founders of the Church of England.'   There is
scarcely a land beneath the sun that has been unaffected by Newton's influence As one of the founders of the Church Missionary Society, he laid his
hand upon all our continents and islands. Through
the personalities of his converts, too, he wielded a
power that is impossible to compute. Take two,
by way of illustration. Newton was the means of

the conversion of Claudius Buchanan and Thomas
Scott. In due time Buchanan carried the gospel
to the East Indies, and wrote a book which led
Adoniram Judson to undertake his historic mission
to Burmah. Scott became one of the most powerful
writers of his time, and, indeed, of all time. Has
not Cardinal Newman confessed that it was Scott's
treatment of the doctrine of the Trinity that preserved his faith, in one of the crises of his soul,
from total shipwreck? And what ought to be said
of Newton's influence on men like Wilberforce and
Cowper, Thornton and Venn? One of our greatest
literary critics has affirmed that the friendship of
Newton saved the intellect of Cowper. 'If, said
Prebendary H. E. Fox, not long ago, 'if Cowper
had never met Newton, the beautiful hymns in the
Olney collection, and that noble poem, "The Task"
—nearest to Milton in English verse—would never
have been written.' Moreover, there are Newton's
own hymns. Wherever, to this day, congregations
join in singing *How Sweet the Name of Jesus
Sounds,*' or '*Glorious Things of Thee are Spoken,*'
or '*One There is Above All Others,*' or '*Amazing
Grace, how Sweet the Sound,*' *there* John Newton
is still at his old task, still making history!

VI

And, all the time, the text hung over the fireplace:
'*Thou shalt remember!*'

'Thou shalt remember that thou wast a bond-man!'

'Thou shalt remember that the Lord thy God redeemed thee!'

From that time forth Newton's treacherous memory troubled him no more. He never again forgot. He never could. He said that when, from the hold of the sinking ship, he cried for mercy, it seemed to him that the Saviour looked into his very soul.

> Sure, never till my latest breath,
>   Can I forget that look;
> It seemed to charge me with His death,
>   Though not a word He spoke.

'I forgot . . .! I soon forgot . . .! This, too, I totally forgot!'

'Thou shalt remember that the Lord thy God redeemed thee!'

'Never till my latest breath can I forget that look!'

The Rev. Richard Cecil, M.A., who afterwards became his biographer, noticing that Newton was beginning to show signs of age, urged him one day to stop preaching and take life easily. 'What!' he replied, 'shall the old African blasphemer stop while he can speak at all?' He could not forget. And he was determined that nobody else should! In order that future generations might know that he was a bondman and had been redeemed, he wrote his own epitaph and expressly directed that this—this and no other—should be erected for him:

JOHN NEWTON,
Clerk,
Once an Infidel and Libertine,
A Servant of Slaves in Africa,
was
by the Mercy of our Lord and Saviour
Jesus Christ,
Preserved, Restored, Pardoned,
And Appointed to Preach the Faith he
had so long laboured to destroy.

No; that treacherous memory of his never betrayed him again! When he was an old, old man,
very near the close of his pilgrimage, William Jay,
of Bath, one day met him in the street. Newton
complained that his powers were failing fast. 'My
memory,' he said, 'is nearly gone; but I remember
two things, that I am a great sinner and that Christ
is a great Saviour!'

*'Thou shalt remember that thou wast a bond-
man in the land of Egypt, and that the Lord thy
God redeemed thee!'*—that was John Newton's
text.

*'My memory is nearly gone; but I remember two
things, that I am a great sinner and that Christ is
a great Saviour!'*—that was John Newton's testimony.

VII

'I forgot . . .! I soon forgot. . .! This, too, I totally forgot!'

'Thou shalt remember, remember, remember!'

Newton liked to think that the memory that had once so basely betrayed him—the memory that, in later years, he had so sternly and perfectly disciplined—would serve him still more delightfully in the life beyond. Cowper died a few years before his friend; and Newton liked to picture to himself their reunion in heaven. He wrote a poem in which he represented himself as grasping Cowper's hand and rapturously addressing him:

> Oh! let thy memory wake! I told thee so;
> I told thee thus would end thy heaviest woe;
> I told thee that thy God would bring thee here,
> And God's own hand would wipe away thy tear,
> While I should claim a mission by thy side;
> I told thee so—for our Emmanuel died.

'Oh! let thy memory wake!'

'I forgot . . .! I soon forgot. . .! This, too, I totally forgot!'

'Thou shalt remember that the Lord thy God redeemed thee!'

Newton felt certain that the joyous recollection of that infinite redemption would be the loftiest bliss of the life that is to be.

XXII

ANDREW FULLER'S TEXT

I

THE Magic Music! What is the Magic Music? Ever since the world began, poets have let their truant fancies play about it, but none of them have told us what it is. They have sung to us of the bells that peal under the sea, of the songs that are heard in the storm, and of sirens that sing on the shore. They have told us of cities that mysteriously rose to the strains of the lyre of Orpheus; and they have told us of cities rendered desolate by the fatal lure of the piper's lute; but none of them have *described* those resistless strains, those bewitching harmonies, that magic and marvellous music! What is it? We must try to find out!

II

Right away down among the swamps of the Red River district, three slaves sit huddled together at the close of a cruel and exhausting day. Two of them are women: the third is Uncle Tom. Seeing that they are too tired to grind their corn, Tom has ground it for them; and, touched by such uncommon sympathy, they have baked his cake for him. Tom sits down by the light of the fire and draws out his Bible, for he has need of comfort.

'What's that?' says one of the women.

'A Bible!' Tom answers.

'Laws a me! And what's that? Read a piece, anyways!' exclaimed the woman, curiously, seeing Tom poring so attentively over it.

'Come unto Me, all ye that labour and are heavy-laden, and I will give you rest!'

'Them's good enough words!' exclaimed the astonished woman. 'Who says 'em?'

And, beginning with those 'good words,' Tom tells her the story of Jesus. But let us change the scene!

We are at the Isle of Wight. And here, in the lovely little church at Newport, is the memorial that Queen Victoria erected to the memory of the Princess Elizabeth. It is by Marochetti, and represents, as Mr. William Canton says, one of the most touching scenes that a sculptor has ever put into marble. It is the figure of a fair young girl in the quaintly pretty dress of the Stuart days. Her eyes are closed; her lips are parted with the last faint sigh. One arm is laid upon her waist; the other has fallen by her side, with the little hand half open —it will never more hold anything. Her left cheek is resting upon an open Bible, and her long ringlets are scattered across the page, but you can read the verse:

'Come unto Me, all ye that labour and are heavy-laden, and I will give you rest!'

Let us change the scene again! We are at Hippo,

in Northern Africa. It is the fifth century. Augustine bends over his desk. Let us glance over his shoulder! What is it that he is writing? 'I have read in Plato and in Cicero,' he says, 'many sayings that are very wise and very beautiful, but I never read in either of them such words as these: *"Come unto Me, all ye that labour and are heavy-laden, and I will give you rest."'*

'*Those are good words!*' says the slave woman, as she listens in astonishment to the reading of Uncle Tom.

'*Those are good words!*' says Queen Victoria, as she selects them for inclusion in the sculptor's masterpiece.

'*Those are good words!*' says Augustine, as he contrasts them with the wealthiest treasures of heathen mines.

Here, then, are words that could pour new hope into the empty heart of a despairing slave; words that could minister consolation and delight to the soul of the world's mightiest sovereign; words that could ravish the mind of an old-world scholar and saint. Here, if anywhere, we have the Magic Music!

'*Come unto Me, all ye that labour and are heavy-laden, and I will give you rest!*'

III

A Slave's text!
A Queen's text!
A Bishop's text!

And Andrew Fuller's Text!

Andrew Fuller made history in three several ways.
To begin at the beginning, he made history by means
of his exquisitely beautiful life at home.   One of
his sons—Andrew G. Fuller, of Wolverhampton—
wrote in his old age a biography of his father.
There were several such works already in existence.
But, in reading them, the second Andrew Fuller felt
that none of them had touched the real secret of his
father's influence and power.   He, therefore, took
his pen, when nearly eighty years of age, and wrote
his book as a filial tribute to the loveliness, the
unselfishness and the nobleness of his father's life
in the home.   Another of Andrew Fuller's sons—
Mr. J. G. Fuller—set up, we have seen, as a printer
at Bristol.   He engaged as his apprentice a young
fellow named William Knibb.   Moved by his
father's spirit, the master was soon the means of
his assistant's conversion.   Having been led to the
Saviour by Mr. Fuller, William Knibb became the
great evangelist of the West Indies and the historic
deliverer of the slaves.   When the glad shout of the
emancipated blacks echoed through the world, nobody thought of Andrew Fuller; yet to Andrew
Fuller's influence that joyous event was directly
traceable.

Andrew Fuller made history by means of one
of the most scrupulously conscientious ministries
that we have on record.   One illustration must
suffice.   As a young man of six and twenty, he was

minister of the little church at Soham. The membership of the church was less than forty; his salary was fifteen pounds a year; and he was far from being happy. The congregation was sharply divided on acute doctrinal questions; several of the leading members treated him with coldness and some with bitterness; and every sermon that he preached was subjected to the most pitiless criticism. At this juncture he was called to the important charge at Kettering. The invitation assured him a much larger congregation, a much larger salary, and absolute unanimity. Yet for two years he hesitated as to the course that he ought to pursue. It seemed to him that the souls of the people at Soham had been committed to his care; and how could he give account of them in the Day of Judgement if he lightly forsook them? The very troubles of the church made it more difficult for his conscience to consent to its abandonment. As Dr. Ryland has remarked, 'many men would risk the fate of an empire with fewer searchings of heart than it cost Andrew Fuller to determine whether he should leave a little dissenting church of less than forty members.' But that was the man! And in that spirit he lived and laboured to the end of his days.

But, most memorably of all, Andrew Fuller made history as one of our great missionary pioneers. When, it has been finely said, when it pleased God to awaken from her slumbers a drowsy and lethargic church, there rang out, from the belfry of the ages,

a clamorous and insistent alarm; and, in that
arousing hour, the hand upon the bell-rope was the
hand of William Carey. Yes, Carey's was the hand
that grasped the rope; but Fuller stood beside him
when he did it. They were partners in the greatest
of all human enterprises. When Carey preached
his famous sermon—the sermon that awoke the
world—Fuller stood beside the pulpit. And Carey
was only able to go to India because Fuller undertook to arouse interest and organise the Church's
resources at home. 'You go down into the mine,'
said Fuller to Carey, 'and we will hold the ropes!'
How well he fulfilled his promise, let his biographers tell. By holding those ropes, Andrew Fuller
made history.

IV

Andrew Fuller was a farmer's son, and, to the end
of his days, he dearly loved the fields. As a boy,
he revelled in the life of the village and the countryside. We get glimpses of him searching for birds'
nests in the woods, killing snakes in the lane, and
sitting with other boys beside the great fire in the
village smithy. Yet, even in those early days, he
was conscious of a hunger in his heart that none
of these pursuits could satisfy. He attended his
mother's church, but the minister did not help him.
Mr. Eve was a representative of that grim and stern
old theology that set the poor boy trembling in every
limb but offered him no refuge from the terrors it

presented. The more he heard, the more miserable he became. In his distress, he collected such books as he could find. He read Bunyan's 'Pilgrim's Progress' and 'Grace Abounding,' and Erskine's 'Gospel Sonnets.' 'I read,' he says, ' and as I read I wept. Indeed, I was almost overcome with weeping, so interesting did the doctrine of eternal salvation appear to me.' But how to make that great salvation his? There lay the problem. He discovered that one of his father's labourers was a very religious man. He followed this man into the fields and stables and barns, hoping that he would drop some word that would dispel the horror of his mind; but no emancipating word was spoken. The quest seemed hopeless. At the age of fifteen he almost abandoned the search. 'I thought,' he says, 'of giving up in despair; why not forget it and take my fill of sin?' But the very idea sent a shudder through all his frame. His heart revolted. 'What!' he said to himself, 'can I give up Christ and hope and heaven?'

Then, one never-to-be-forgotten day, his ears were ravished by the Magic Music! He heard the text :

'Come unto Me, all ye that labour and are heavy-laden, and I will give you rest!'

He looked away from self, his son tells us; and fixed his eyes upon a crucified Saviour; his guilt and fears began to dissolve like the snows of winter under the silent influence of spring-time warmth.

He was in such dire extremity that, whether it accorded with the teachings of Mr. Eve or not, he determined to venture everything upon Christ!

'*Come unto me!*' said the Matchless Music.

'*I must!*' his soul made answer. '*I must and I will! Yes, I will, I will! I trust my soul—my lost and sinful soul—in His hands! I come, I come! And if I perish, I perish!*' The words are copied from his own account of that memorable experience.

'*Come unto Me, all ye that labour and are heavy-laden, and I will give you rest!*'

He came; and, in coming, he found the rest that was promised, the rest he had so diligently sought. 'I should have found it sooner,' he says, 'if I had not entertained the notion of my having no warrant to come to Christ without some previous qualification. I mention this,' he adds, 'because it may be the case with others who may be kept in darkness and despondency by such views much longer than I was.'

V

During the years that followed, Andrew Fuller had his full share of trouble. Whilst he lay ill in one room, his daughter, a little girl of six, died in the room adjoining.

'I heard a whispering,' he says, 'and then all were silent. All were silent! But all is well. I feel reconciled to God. I called my family around my bed. I sat up and prayed with them as well as I

could. I bowed my head and worshipped a *taking*
as well as a *giving* God!'

Some time afterwards, Mrs. Fuller lost her
reason. In her frenzy she fancied that he was not
her husband, but an impostor, who had entered the
house and taken all that belonged to her. She regarded him as her bitterest enemy and made every
effort to escape. She had to be watched night and
day. Just before her death, however, a sudden
calm stole over her. 'I was weeping,' Mr. Fuller
says, 'and the sight of my tears seemed to awaken
her recollection. Fixing her eyes upon me, she
exclaimed, "Why, are you indeed my husband?"
"Indeed, my dear, I am!" She then drew near and
kissed me several times. My heart dissolved with a
mixture of grief and joy. Her senses were restored,
and she talked as rationally as ever.' A fortnight
later she laid a little child in the father's arms and
then passed quietly away.

Then again, her eldest boy proved wayward and
gave him serious trouble. He ran away to sea. It
was reported that, as a result of a misadventure,
he had received three hundred lashes, and had died
under the punishment. 'Oh,' cried the father, when
he heard of it, 'this is *heart* trouble! My boy, my
boy! He cried and I heard him not! O Absalom!
my son! my son! Would God I had died for thee,
my son, my son!'

It turned out, however, that the rumour was false.
Robert was still alive, and the letters that his father

wrote him are among the tenderest and most persuasive in our literature. There is every reason to believe that their pleadings had the effect that the father most desired. 'I was exceedingly intimate with Robert,' wrote a shipmate long afterwards. 'We freely opened our minds to each other. He was a very pleasing youth and became a true Christian man.' The news of his death, however, was a terrible blow to Mr. Fuller. On the Sunday following its reception, he broke down completely in the pulpit, and the whole congregation wept with him.

But, through all the clash of feeling and the tumult of emotion, the bells were ringing under the sea. The Magic Music never ceased.

'Come unto Me, all ye that labour and are heavy-laden, and I will give you rest!'

That rest was never broken. When he lay dying at the last, he called Dr. Ryland to receive his final testimony. 'I have no other hope of salvation,' he said, 'than through the atonement of my Lord and Saviour. With this hope I can go into eternity with composure.'

'I will give you rest!'

'I go into eternity with composure!'

Rest! Composure! So steadfastly was the promise kept to the very, very last!

VI

As a boy, I came under the influence of a fine

old clergyman—Canon Hoare, the rector of Holy Trinity, Tunbridge Wells—a man very highly esteemed in the South of England. I can see him now, tall, stately and grey, my beau ideal of all that a minister should be. In his study there hung a very beautiful and telling picture. It represented a shipwreck from which one life was being saved. In confidential moments, Canon Hoare would tell the story of the picture. It seems that, years ago, a very wealthy man called to arrange with him about his burial-place. The Canon walked round the churchyard with him, and, after inspecting several possible positions, the gentleman at last selected the spot in which he wished his bones to rest. This business completed, they paused for a second or two, listening to the birds, and then the Canon turned to his companion and said:

'Well, now; you have chosen a resting-place for your *body*. Have you yet found a resting-place for your *soul?*'

There was silence for a moment, and then, turning full upon the Canon, the gentleman exclaimed:

'You are the first man who ever asked me that question!'

It set him thinking. He sought and found the resting-place, the only resting-place, Andrew Fuller's resting-place; and he sent the Canon the picture as a token of his gratitude. He felt that *his* was the life that had been saved from shipwreck.

'The Matchless Music!'

'A Resting-place for the Soul!'

'Come unto Me, all ye that labour and are heavy-laden, and I will give you rest!'

He who has heard that music, and found that resting-place, will smile at all the buffetings of time and pass into eternity with composure.

XXIII

STEPHEN GRELLET'S TEXT

I

A RESTLESS and adventurous Quaker was Stephen
Grellet. He yearned to live to the age of Methuselah,
and, had his wish been granted, he would have made
good use of every moment of his time. The marvel
is, however, that he lived to be eighty-two. He was
nearly hanged to a lamp-post by infuriated revolutionists in Paris; he was twice faced with death by
drowning—once in a swollen mill-race and once at
a flooded ford; he twice fell into the hands of pirates
from whose cutlasses he had good reason to expect
a hasty despatch; and, in the course of his tireless
travels amidst populations that were being ravaged
by plagues and pestilences, he was laid low again
and again. More than once he gave specific instructions concerning the burial of his body. But
each time he rose from his fevered couch and continued his tireless pilgrimage. He passed from
country to country with as little concern as some men
feel in passing from village to village. He learned
language after language in order that he might
preach the Word in every hole and corner of the

earth. He stood before Emperors and Kings, speaking to crowned heads with the naturalness and ease with which he addressed the children at home. He found his way into prisons and workhouses; into slave camps and thieves' kitchens; he lost no opportunity of preaching to all kinds and conditions of men the words of everlasting life. His is one of the most remarkable evangelistic careers on record.

II

He yearned to live as long as Methuselah; but he discovered that he could live longer still. That discovery is, in a word, the explanation of his life. Let him tell his own story. 'One evening,' he says, 'I was walking in the fields alone, my mind being under no kind of religious concern, nor in the least excited by anything I had heard or thought of.' Suddenly, explain it how you may, the solitudes of that vast American forest declined any longer to be dumb. They became vocal with wondrous speech. The wayward winds and the rustling leaves were all whispering and caroling and shouting and echoing the same wonderful word. 'I was arrested,' he says, 'by what seemed to be an awful voice proclaiming the word, *"Eternity! Eternity! Eternity!"* It reached my very soul—my whole man shook—it brought me, like Saul, to the ground. The great depravity and sinfulness of my heart were set open before me. . . . After this, I spent most of my time

in retirement. I began to read the Bible. O, what
sweetness did I then feel! It was indeed a memorable day. I was like one introduced into a new
world; the creation, and all things around me, bore
a different aspect—my heart glowed with love to all.
The awfulness of that visitation can never cease to
be remembered with peculiar interest and gratitude,
as long as I have the use of my mental faculties. I
have been as one plucked from a burning house—
rescued from the brink of a horrible pit¹ . . . How
can I set forth the fullness of heavenly joy that filled
me? I saw that there was One that was able to
save me. I saw Him to be the Lamb of God that
taketh away the sins of the world. I felt faith in
His atoning blood. Floods of tears of joy and
gratitude gave vent to the fullness of my heart!'
And all through one word—'a word that reached
my very soul, shook my whole man, and brought me
to the ground!—that word *Eternity!*'

Eternity!
Eternity!

III

Eternity!
Eternity!

The very word is the stateliest cathedral of
human speech. It is the transcendent triumph of
articulation. It stands among the few real sublimities of our vocabulary. It is one of those mag-
nificences of language that defy all definition, one

of those splendours of expression that leave nothing
to be said.

> Oh, the clanging bells of Time!
>   How their changes rise and fall;
> But in undertone sublime,
>   Sounding clearly through them all
> Is a voice that must be heard,
>   As our moments onward flee;
> And it speaketh aye one word,—
>   Eternity! Eternity!

That insistent voice is the voice that Stephen
Grellet heard in the leafy solitudes that memorable
evening. *'Eternity! Eternity! Eternity!'* The
word falls upon the ear like the booming of the
ocean on the crags along the coast. It rings and
echoes and reverberates and resounds through all the
intricate avenues and the tortuous corridors of the
soul. The whole being trembles at its utterance as
the abbey shudders to the organ's diapason. Every
faculty is awed into stillness; the soul is hushed into
worship. The word has all the music of the spheres
within its syllables; and, when it has been spoken,
all attempts at amplification or explanation become
pitiful impertinences.

Eternity!
Eternity!

IV

Eternity!
Eternity!
The classic use of the word occurs in Mrs. Beecher

Stowe's historic masterpiece. Poor Uncle Tom, having fallen into the hands of the wretched and brutal Legree, had been thrashed within an inch of his life. He lay bleeding, and writhing in anguish, in the old slave-shed. But his soul was not in the shed. For, as the solemn light of dawn—the angelic glory of the morning star—looks in through the rude window, Tom thinks of the Bright and Morning Star. He ponders on the Great White Throne, with its ever-radiant rainbow; the white-robed multitude, with voices as many waters; the crowns, the palms, the harps; these may all break upon his vision before that sun shall set again. And, therefore, without shuddering or trembling, he hears the voice of his persecutor:

'How would ye like to be tied to a tree, and have a slow fire lit up around ye?' asks Legree. 'Wouldn't that be pleasant, eh, Tom?'

'Mas'r, says Tom, 'I know ye can do dreadful things, but'—he stretched himself upward and clasped his hands—'but after ye've killed the body, there ain't no more ye can do. And, oh! there's all *Eternity* to come after that!'

Eternity!

'*Eternity!*' exclaims Mrs. Beecher Stowe, 'the word thrills through the black man's soul with light and power as he utters it; it thrills through the sinner's soul, too, like the bite of a scorpion.'

Eternity!
Eternity!

V

Eternity!
Eternity!
It is one of the overpowering immensities of our
faith, and we preachers must make the most of it.
The people are sick and tired of trifles. The day
of catch-penny titles and silly subjects is as dead as
the dodo. It ought never to have dawned. It is a
page in church history over which every true minister of the New Testament will blush whenever he
comes upon it. The man who announces as his theme
a subject that is beneath the dignity of the eternal
harmonies can never have heard the music of the
choir invisible. He can never have seen the Lord
high and lifted up. He can never have heard the
seraphs that cry continually: 'Holy, Holy, Holy is
the Lord of Hosts; the whole earth is full of His
glory!' The lips that have been touched with the
glowing coal from the altar can never again be lent
to ecclesiastical frivolity. It is wrong; it is wicked;
it is shameful. And, to quote a famous but sinister
phrase, 'it is not only a crime, it is a blunder.' For
the people are impatient of trivialities. The hearts
of men are hungry for the most stupendous themes.
They like great preaching. The big subjects draw
the big crowds. Little children amidst city squalor
love to put the sea-shells to their ears because in them
they catch the murmur of fathomless seas and limitless oceans; and children of a larger growth turn

from much that is sordid in their environment to the preacher who helps them to hear the music of the infinite.

Eternity!
Eternity!

'
VI

Eternity!
Eternity!

The best illustration of my theme occurs in the life of Dr. Thomas Chalmers. It is a dramatic page in a wonderful spiritual experience. Let me briefly marshal the facts. As a mere boy, having matriculated at twelve, become a divinity student at fifteen, and been licensed to preach at nineteen, Chalmers becomes a minister at Kilmany. He devotes himself to mathematics. On Sundays he thunders to decent Presbyterians against murder and adultery; and during the week he seeks to prepare himself to succeed Professor Playfair in the Mathematical Chair of Edinburgh University. He writes a pamphlet, in which he says: 'The author of this pamphlet can assert from what to him is the highest of all authority—the authority of his own experience—that, after the satisfactory discharge of his parish duties, a minister may enjoy five days in the week of uninterrupted leisure for the prosecution of any science in which his taste may dispose him to engage.' Then follow his illness, his marvellous conversion, and his new ministry. Has Scotland ever known a life more rich in spiritual influence or more fruitful of evangelistic fervour? And in the course of that historic ministry, in a debate before the General Assembly of the Church of Scotland, Chalmers' early pamphlet is quoted in support of the low views it advocates. Chalmers is stung to the quick. He rises and makes one of his very greatest speeches. And, in closing, he exclaims: 'Yes, sir, I penned it, strangely blinded that I was! I aspired in those days to be a professor of mathematics. But what, sir, is the object of mathematical science? Magnitude, and the proportion of magnitude! But in those days, sir, I had forgotten two magnitudes—I thought not of the littleness of *Time,* and I recklessly thought not of the greatness of *Eternity!*'

Eternity!
Eternity!

VII

Eternity!
Eternity!

I recently took a long, long railway journey. Through a thousand miles of civilisation, a thousand miles of desert, and a thousand miles of bush, the train bore me to a part of this vast continent in which I found myself surrounded by trees that were entirely new to me, and by flowers such as I had never seen before. I freely expressed my admiration, and, when the time came to commence my homeward journey, I found among the mementoes with which I was presented a beautiful bunch of everlastings. *A Bunch of Everlastings!* It seems to me I have this morning been gathering just such a bouquet. Here is Stephen Grellet listening to the great word that rings through the silence of the forest, *'Eternity! Eternity! Eternity!'* Here is Uncle Tom uttering the same word with strange and wonderful effects: *'Eternity!'* Here is Dr. Chalmers confessing that the mistakes of his life lay in his forgetting the greatness of *Eternity!* The list could be indefinitely continued; the valleys are full of everlastings. 'That night,' says Ebenezer Erskine, in recording in the pages of his diary the greatest spiritual crisis that he ever knew, 'that night I got my head out of Time into *Eternity!'* 'The vastness of the word *Eternity* was impressed upon me,' says Andrew Bonar in his diary; and, a few months later, he says again, 'I strive to keep the feeling of *Eternity* always before me!' 'Gentlemen,' exclaims old Rabbi Duncan to his students as he dismisses them at the end of the year's work, 'many will be wishing you a Happy New Year. Your old tutor wishes you a happy *Eternity!'*

Eternity!
Eternity!

VIII

Eternity!
Eternity!

It is good, as Stephen Grellet discovered on that memorable evening, to wander at times into the fields and the forests.   To-day I have been out into the fields that are boundless, and, as the fruits of my stroll, I have brought back—

A Bunch of Everlastings!

BIBLIOLIFE

Old Books Deserve a New Life
www.bibliolife.com

Did you know that you can get most of our titles in our trademark **EasyScript**™ print format? **EasyScript**™ provides readers with a larger than average typeface, for a reading experience that's easier on the eyes.

Did you know that we have an ever-growing collection of books in many languages?

Order online:
www.bibliolife.com/store

Or to exclusively browse our **EasyScript**™ collection:
www.bibliogrande.com

At BiblioLife, we aim to make knowledge more accessible by making thousands of titles available to you – quickly and affordably.

Contact us:
BiblioLife
PO Box 21206
Charleston, SC 29413

CPSIA information can be obtained at www.ICGtesting.com
Printed in the USA
LVOW110354180512

282273LV00007BA/16/P